# Mastering Linkerd
## A Complete Guide to Service Mesh Deployment and Management

Nova Trex

© 2024 by Wang Press. All rights reserved.

No part of this publication may be reproduced, distributed, or transmitted in any form or by any means, including photocopying, recording, or other electronic or mechanical methods, without the prior written permission of the publisher, except in the case of brief quotations embodied in critical reviews and certain other noncommercial uses permitted by copyright law.

Published by Wang Press

For permissions and other inquiries, write to:
P.O. Box 3132, Framingham, MA 01701, USA

# Contents

**1 Introduction to Service Mesh and Linkerd** — 9
- 1.1 Understanding Service Mesh .............. 9
- 1.2 Overview of Linkerd .................. 14
- 1.3 Comparing Linkerd with Other Service Meshes ..... 17
- 1.4 Core Components of Linkerd .............. 21
- 1.5 History and Development of Linkerd .......... 25

**2 Architecture of Linkerd** — 29
- 2.1 Linkerd Control Plane ................. 29
- 2.2 Linkerd Data Plane .................. 33
- 2.3 Sidecar Pattern in Linkerd .............. 37
- 2.4 Service Discovery and Routing ............. 41
- 2.5 Configuration and Customization ........... 45
- 2.6 Scalability and Fault Tolerance ............ 50

**3 Installing and Configuring Linkerd** — 55
- 3.1 System Requirements for Linkerd ........... 55
- 3.2 Installing Linkerd CLI ................ 59
- 3.3 Setting Up Linkerd on Kubernetes ........... 63

|     |     |                                          |     |
| --- | --- | ---------------------------------------- | --- |
|     | 3.4 | Verifying the Installation               | 68  |
|     | 3.5 | Configuring Linkerd for Your Environment | 72  |
|     | 3.6 | Updating and Maintaining Linkerd         | 77  |

## 4 Core Features of Linkerd   83

|     |                                      |     |
| --- | ------------------------------------ | --- |
| 4.1 | Traffic Routing and Load Balancing   | 83  |
| 4.2 | Observability and Metrics Collection | 87  |
| 4.3 | Automatic mTLS Encryption            | 91  |
| 4.4 | Service Latency and Health Checks    | 95  |
| 4.5 | Advanced Traffic Control             | 99  |

## 5 Securing Services with Linkerd   105

|     |                                           |     |
| --- | ----------------------------------------- | --- |
| 5.1 | Understanding mTLS in Linkerd             | 105 |
| 5.2 | Identity Management and Security Policies | 110 |
| 5.3 | Configuring Network Policies              | 115 |
| 5.4 | Certificate Management and Rotation       | 120 |
| 5.5 | Auditing and Security Monitoring          | 124 |
| 5.6 | Handling External Threats                 | 129 |

## 6 Traffic Management in Linkerd   135

|     |                                       |     |
| --- | ------------------------------------- | --- |
| 6.1 | Traffic Splitting and Canary Releases | 135 |
| 6.2 | Request Routing and Service Discovery | 139 |
| 6.3 | Load Balancing Algorithms             | 142 |
| 6.4 | Circuit Breaking for Resilience       | 146 |
| 6.5 | Managing Latency and Timeouts         | 149 |
| 6.6 | Advanced Traffic Policies             | 153 |

## 7 Monitoring and Observability with Linkerd   157

|     |                                     |     |
| --- | ----------------------------------- | --- |
| 7.1 | Metrics Collection and Dashboarding | 158 |

7.2 Tracing and Logging . . . . . . . . . . . . . . . . . . . . 160
7.3 Alerting and Notifications . . . . . . . . . . . . . . . . . 163
7.4 Granular Observability with Prometheus . . . . . . . . 166
7.5 Visualizing Service Health with Grafana . . . . . . . . . 169
7.6 Monitoring Service Dependencies . . . . . . . . . . . . 173

## 8  Linkerd Performance and Scalability          179
8.1 Optimizing Linkerd for High Performance . . . . . . . 180
8.2 Horizontal and Vertical Scaling Techniques . . . . . . . 184
8.3 Resource Management and Quotas . . . . . . . . . . . 188
8.4 Handling Large Scale Deployments . . . . . . . . . . . 192
8.5 Performance Benchmarking and Testing . . . . . . . . 197
8.6 Improving Response Times and Throughput . . . . . . 201

## 9  Best Practices for Linkerd in Production     207
9.1 Preparing for Production Deployment . . . . . . . . . 208
9.2 Managing Configuration and Secrets . . . . . . . . . . 212
9.3 Ensuring High Availability . . . . . . . . . . . . . . . . 216
9.4 Continuous Integration and Deployment . . . . . . . . 220
9.5 Monitoring and Incident Response . . . . . . . . . . . 224
9.6 Backup and Disaster Recovery . . . . . . . . . . . . . . 228

## 10  Future of Linkerd and Service Mesh Ecosystems    233
10.1 Evolving Trends in Service Mesh Technologies . . . . . 234
10.2 Future Roadmap for Linkerd . . . . . . . . . . . . . . . 239
10.3 Integration with Emerging Technologies . . . . . . . . 243
10.4 Multi-Cloud Strategies for Linkerd . . . . . . . . . . . . 248
10.5 Role of Linkerd in DevOps and SRE . . . . . . . . . . . 251
10.6 Community and Open Source Contributions . . . . . . 256

CONTENTS

# Introduction

In the rapidly evolving landscape of modern software development, the demand for highly resilient, scalable, and manageable cloud-native applications has never been more pronounced. Organizations adopting microservices architectures face increasing complexities related to service-to-service communications, observability, and security. This is where service meshes like Linkerd have emerged as crucial tools, providing a sophisticated framework to manage network functions such as service discovery, load balancing, failure recovery, and telemetry collection — all indispensable for effective service orchestration.

Among a variety of service mesh solutions available today, Linkerd is distinguished by its lightweight design, operational simplicity, and powerful features targeted at overcoming the challenges inherent in distributed systems. As a CNCF project, Linkerd is open source and benefits from a vibrant community contributing to its continuous improvement, making it an attractive option for organizations seeking enterprise-grade service mesh capabilities without the weight of overly complex solutions.

This book, "Mastering Linkerd: A Complete Guide to Service Mesh Deployment and Management," is meticulously crafted to provide readers with an in-depth comprehension of Linkerd's architecture, installation procedures, configuration options, and recommended practices for deploying it in production environments. The content deeply explores how Linkerd enhances security with features like automatic mutual TLS (mTLS), manages complex traffic routing, and offers comprehensive monitoring and observability, thus equipping practitioners with the essential tools and knowledge to maximize Linkerd's potential.

In addition to foundational concepts, this book presents advanced topics including the optimization of Linkerd for performance, strategies for horizontal and vertical scaling, and methodologies for deploying Linkerd across large-scale, complex production systems. Such insights empower readers to tailor Linkerd solutions specifically to their organizational needs, ensuring optimal performance, scalability, and resilience in cloud-native applications.

Moreover, this book anticipates the future trajectory of Linkerd and service mesh technologies at large, pondering the implications of emerging trends, new feature sets, and potential influences on cloud computing's continual evolution. Through an amalgamation of theoretical exploration and practical instruction, "Mastering Linkerd" targets readers who are either new to the arena of service meshes or those well-versed with the technology but keen on mastering its nuances for sophisticated implementations.

In conclusion, as the drive for robust and adaptable service management models grows, mastering Linkerd becomes an indispensable skill for developers, system architects, and IT operations teams alike. This book is structured to serve as the ultimate guide, fostering the proficiency needed to deftly implement, manage, and innovate within the Linkerd framework, strategically positioning its readers at the forefront of modern application delivery and infrastructure management.

# Chapter 1

# Introduction to Service Mesh and Linkerd

A service mesh is a dedicated infrastructure layer that manages service-to-service communication in microservices architectures, providing essential capabilities such as traffic management, security, and observability. Linkerd, as a prominent service mesh, offers a lightweight and efficient solution tailored to the needs of cloud-native applications. This chapter aims to provide a foundational understanding of the concept of service mesh and the role of Linkerd within this framework. It covers the fundamental aspects of service meshes, Linkerd's features, comparisons with other service mesh solutions, and an overview of its core components and development history.

## 1.1 Understanding Service Mesh

The concept of a service mesh represents a transformative approach to managing the complex interactions that occur within modern, cloud-native architectures. This infrastructure layer is embedded within the architecture, functioning seamlessly to manage service-to-service communication among microservices. By encapsulating fundamental elements such as traffic management, security, and observability, a service mesh simplifies the operational complexities of microservices.

The necessity of a service mesh arises from the limitations of traditional approaches to service communication, which often entail rigid configurations, scaling issues, and inconsistency in handling service interactions. These limitations are especially pronounced when deploying highly distributed architectures characterized by numerous microservices that necessitate dynamic and resilient inter-service communication.

**Traffic Management** within a service mesh environment encompasses a range of features designed to enhance the efficiency and reliability of service communication. Typical features include intelligent routing, load balancing, and traffic splitting, enabling refined control over the service interaction pathways. At its core, intelligent routing is vital for directing requests to optimal service instances based on various criteria such as load, latency, or geographical proximity. This routing is often achieved through sophisticated algorithms or declarative configurations defined within the service mesh framework.

In contrast, traditional load balancers typically operate at the ingress level of a service ecosystem, dealing with North-South traffic (inbound and outbound). A service mesh, however, is acutely concerned with East-West traffic (internal system communications), offering fine-grained control to optimize interactions within the microservice architecture. The capability for **traffic splitting** facilitates progressive delivery strategies, such as canary deployments and blue-green deployments, which are crucial for minimizing risk during updates and ensuring continuity in service availability.

The following code snippet illustrates a basic YAML configuration for routing traffic in a service mesh, employing a common service mesh implementation like Istio:

```
apiVersion: networking.istio.io/v1alpha3
kind: VirtualService
metadata:
  name: myservice
spec:
  hosts:
  - "myservice.example.com"
  http:
  - match:
```

## 1.1. UNDERSTANDING SERVICE MESH

```
    - uri:
        prefix: "/v1"
      route:
      - destination:
          host: v1.yourservice.svc.cluster.local
          subset: v1
    - match:
      - uri:
          prefix: "/v2"
      route:
      - destination:
          host: v2.yourservice.svc.cluster.local
          subset: v2
```

In this example, a service mesh is configured to direct requests to different versions of a service based on URI patterns, implementing a version-based routing strategy fundamental to microservices upgrades and experimentation.

**Security** is an intrinsic benefit of implementing a service mesh, enhancing the overall security posture of microservice communications. With a service mesh, each service-to-service communication can be encrypted and authenticated through mutual TLS (mTLS). This encryption ensures that data in transit is protected against interception, while authentication verifies service identities before communication occurs, significantly mitigating the risk of impersonation and unauthorized access.

Additionally, service meshes provide security policies that can be defined and applied consistently across services, alleviating the need for developers to implement security features individually within each service. These policies enable the definition of permissible communication paths, control access at the level of individual microservices, and enforce robust authorization models. Consequently, security is baked into the architectural infrastructure, promoting compliance and consistency.

To illustrate a simple setup for enabling mTLS in a service mesh:

```
apiVersion: policy.linkerd.io/v1beta1
kind: ServerAuthorization
metadata:
  name: myservice-authz
spec:
  server:
    name: myservice
  client:
    meshTLS:
```

```
    identities:
    - '*'
```

This configuration for Linkerd demonstrates how to enforce mutual TLS for a service, authorizing any client within the service mesh to communicate securely with 'myservice'.

**Observability** is a critical advantage provided by service meshes, bringing enhanced insights and visibility into microservice interactions. Observability tools embedded within a service mesh give operators the ability to monitor service performance, detect anomalies, and trace service dependencies across a distributed environment. Service meshes facilitate comprehensive monitoring through metrics collection, distributed tracing, and logging without requiring source code modification.

Metrics collected include service latency, error rates, and request volumes, allowing operators to gain a quantitative understanding of service performance. Distributed tracing further enriches the observability framework, enabling the correlation of requests as they propagate through service chains, capturing a complete picture of service dependencies and interactions. These features combine to empower operators to troubleshoot issues effectively and implement optimizations based on empirical data.

Below is an example of a Prometheus configuration that can be utilized within a service mesh context to scrape metrics data:

```
scrape_configs:
  - job_name: 'linkerd'
    metrics_path: /metrics
    scheme: https
    tls_config:
      ca_file: /etc/prometheus/certs/ca.crt
      cert_file: /etc/prometheus/certs/prometheus.crt
      key_file: /etc/prometheus/certs/prometheus.key
    static_configs:
      - targets:
        - 'linkerd-controller:9090'
        - 'linkerd-proxy:4191'
```

This configuration file directs Prometheus to securely scrape metrics from Linkerd components, ensuring that critical performance data is available for analysis.

Service mesh implementations, such as Linkerd, Istio, and Consul Connect, share the common objective of facilitating these elements of traffic management, security, and observability while differing in design philosophy, technical capabilities, and resource requirements. The choice of a particular service mesh thus depends on the specific constraints and goals of the deployment environment, including factors such as ease of installation, configurability, performance overhead, and integration with existing tools.

Conceptually, a service mesh may include the following architectural components:

- **Sidecar Proxies:** These are lightweight network proxies deployed alongside each service instance. They intercept and manage all incoming and outgoing network traffic, implementing the data plane of the service mesh. By managing traffic at this level, sidecars enable the decoupling of operational concerns from business logic.

- **Control Plane:** This component is responsible for orchestrating the sidecar proxies, distributing configurations, and enforcing policies across the mesh. The control plane interacts with operators and administrators through APIs or user interfaces, often featuring dashboards, to streamline service management.

- **Service Mesh Interface:** A common specification to ensure compatibility and interoperability among different service mesh implementations, promoting a standardized approach to defining service meshes.

Service meshes are engineered to be highly extensible, allowing organizations to tailor the components and policies to their precise operational needs. Such flexibility is critical as microservices architectures continue to evolve, requiring adaptive infrastructures capable of supporting complex service interactions while maintaining high levels of security and observability.

As cloud-native applications continue to proliferate, the importance of efficient and effective service management grows concomitantly. The adoption of a service mesh is a strategic decision that can significantly enhance the robustness, security, and transparency of a microservices ecosystem, setting the stage for scalable and agile application delivery.

## 1.2 Overview of Linkerd

Linkerd is a pioneering project in the realm of service meshes, specifically designed to provide robust and efficient solutions for managing service-to-service communication within cloud-native environments. As an open-source service mesh, Linkerd brings simplicity, performance, and security to microservice architectures. By implementing critical aspects such as observability, reliability, and security, Linkerd addresses the inherent challenges faced by distributed systems.

Linkerd fundamentally operates by deploying proxies alongside each instance of a service. These proxies intercept all incoming and outgoing calls, providing a layer of transparency and control over the communication between services. This deployment pattern, known as the sidecar pattern, enables Linkerd to manage network traffic without requiring modifications to individual services. It effectively abstracts the complexities of service-to-service communication away from application-level logic, streamlining operations and allowing developers to focus on core application functionality.

The primary motivation behind Linkerd's design philosophy is its emphasis on simplicity and lightweight features, contrasting with the more comprehensive and complex service mesh solutions like Istio. Linkerd prioritizes ease of setup, intuitive operation, and optimal performance overhead. This focus is especially beneficial for teams seeking to minimize complexity while still gaining critical service mesh functionalities. Linkerd provides sensible defaults that allow for quick and easy adoption, suitable for a range of deployment sizes and technical abilities.

Among the various components of Linkerd, the **control plane** and **data plane** form its core architecture. The control plane is responsible for managing the configurations and policies that determine how the data plane operates. In Linkerd's architecture:

- **Control Plane:** This consists of several components that handle the global operations of the service mesh. The control plane is responsible for interpreting user-specified configuration, distributing these configurations to the sidecar proxies, and managing component interactions within the mesh. Key functionalities of the control plane include service discovery, load balancing, routing, metrics aggregation, and tracing functionalities.

- **Data Plane:** The data plane is composed of the Linkerd proxy instances that run alongside each service. This includes processing network requests, enforcing access control policies, collecting and reporting metrics, and maintaining secure communication via mTLS. The Linkerd proxy is written in Rust, which allows for high performance by utilizing Rust's memory safety and thread concurrency features without incurring significant computational costs.

Linkerd provides several essential features that augment the capabilities of a Kubernetes-based microservices architecture. These include:

**Observability and Metrics:** Linkerd enables comprehensive observability by providing out-of-the-box operational insights into service behavior. Metrics such as request count, success rate, and latency are automatically collected. These metrics are exposed in a format compatible with Prometheus, enabling seamless integration with broader observability platforms. The following configuration enables Prometheus to scrape and visualize these metrics:

```
scrape_configs:
  - job_name: 'linkerd'
    static_configs:
      - targets: ['linkerd-proxy-admin:4191', 'linkerd-controller:8084']
```

Linkerd also supports distributed tracing, allowing operators to understand the request flow through different services, thereby assisting with debugging and performance tuning. The automatically generated Grafana dashboards make it easy to visualize these metrics, offering comprehensive insights into the operation of microservices.

**Security:** Security is a core feature embedded in Linkerd's design through its automatic end-to-end mTLS implementation. By using mTLS, Linkerd authenticates and encrypts all network communications between services, ensuring data integrity and confidentiality. The secure communication provided by Linkerd's automatic certificate management relieves developers from the incessant task of managing certificates manually. Below is an example of how to set up a Namespace policy within Linkerd to handle mTLS:

```
apiVersion: policy.linkerd.io/v1beta1
kind: AuthorizationPolicy
metadata:
  name: default-deny
  namespace: production
spec:
  targetRef:
    kind: Namespace
    name: production
  allow:
  - principals:
    - "*"
    network:
      passThrough: true
  deny:
  - principals:
    - "unauthenticated"
```

This policy ensures that only authenticated services within the 'production' namespace can communicate, thereby enhancing the security posture of microservices within the mesh.

**Traffic Management:** With its rich set of traffic management capabilities, Linkerd gives operators the control needed to efficiently route and manage traffic between services. Among these capabilities are traffic splitting for facilitating progressive deployments, such as canary and blue-green deployments, and sophisticated failover mechanisms. Linkerd employs a declarative model to manage routing rules, often written in custom resource definitions (CRDs) within Kubernetes. Below is an example of how to define a simple traffic split for progressive delivery:

```
apiVersion: split.smi-spec.io/v1alpha1
kind: TrafficSplit
metadata:
  name: canary-release
  namespace: default
spec:
  service: myservice
  backends:
  - service: myservice-stable
    weight: "80"
  - service: myservice-canary
    weight: "20"
```

In this example, 'myservice' is split between the stable and canary versions, with 80% of incoming traffic directed to the stable service and 20% to the canary service, enabling safe deployment validations.

Linkerd is built on a foundation of cloud-native principles, enhancing its integration capabilities with Kubernetes environments. This seamless integration allows Linkerd to leverage native Kubernetes features such as namespaces, automatic sidecar injection, and network policies, effectively simplifying management and operational complexities.

The positioning of Linkerd as a pragmatic lightweight service mesh solution is often emphasized by its design decisions that focus on user experience and performance optimizations. By prioritizing performance, Linkerd is able to operate with substantially lower resource overhead, making it suitable for environments sensitive to computational expense, like resource-constrained or latency-critical applications.

Through its active community and continuous development, Linkerd has evolved to address emerging requirements from real-world use cases. It stands as a compelling choice for organizations aiming to strengthen their infrastructure's reliability, visibility, and security without succumbing to the additional operational burden associated with more feature-rich service meshes.

As devops teams and architects increasingly adopt cloud-native paradigms, Linkerd serves a pivotal role in simplifying the service communication layer. Empowering developers to implement robust service-to-service communication transparently, Linkerd embodies the core tenets of what a modern service mesh should deliver, tailoring its solutions to meet evolving microservice challenges with precision and reliability.

## 1.3 Comparing Linkerd with Other Service Meshes

Linkerd, as a leading implementation in the landscape of service meshes, offers a distinctive approach compared to other popular service mesh solutions such as Istio, Consul Connect, and AWS App Mesh. Each service mesh provides a tailored solution to address specific challenges within microservice architectures, varying in feature set, integration capabilities, and operational complexity. This section delves into a comparative analysis between Linkerd and its counterparts, examining the unique benefits and considerations associated with each option, delving into their architecture, deployment complexity, performance, and community support.

One fundamental aspect that distinguishes Linkerd from other service meshes like Istio and Consul Connect is its emphasis on simplicity and lightweight design. Linkerd's development philosophy is centered on delivering a service mesh that is straightforward to deploy and manage, with a focus on providing essential features without the complexity that often accompanies more feature-replete solutions like Istio.

**Architecture and Design Philosophy:** At the core of Linkerd's architecture is the utilization of lightweight proxies written in Rust, which significantly contributes to its high performance and minimal resource consumption. The choice of Rust provides several advantages, such as memory safety without a garbage collector and concurrency handling capabilities that are highly beneficial in latency-sensitive environments. In contrast, Istio's design incorporates more comprehensive capabilities through Envoy proxies, which can be more resource-intensive and complex to configure.

Consul Connect, on the other hand, integrates directly with HashiCorp's Consul for service discovery and configuration management, leveraging Consul's strong infrastructure network capabilities. This integration positions Consul Connect favorably for organizations already invested in HashiCorp's ecosystem, ensuring ease of integration and consistency across their operational stack.

**Deployment Complexity and Ease of Use:** Linkerd's deployment process is intentionally crafted to be as seamless as possible, featuring automatic proxy injection and a set of default configurations that simplify early adoption. This focus on user experience enables teams to quickly establish Linkerd in their environment with minimal manual intervention. Here is an example of deploying Linkerd with a simple command-line interface:

```
linkerd install | kubectl apply -f -
```

In contrast, Istio's deployment can entail a more involved setup due to its numerous configuration options and potential integrations. While this comprehensive configurability is advantageous for advanced use cases demanding intricate policies and routing logic, it can also pose a steep learning curve for teams new to service meshes.

## 1.3. COMPARING LINKERD WITH OTHER SERVICE MESHES

AWS App Mesh augments its service offerings with AWS's rich feature set, providing tight integration with other AWS services. This integration adds value for teams utilizing AWS for their infrastructure by offering managed service capabilities that minimize operational overhead. However, this dependency might limit its applicability to organizations operating multi-cloud environments.

**Performance and Resource Utilization:** Performance remains a chief concern in deploying a service mesh, with potential impacts on latency and throughput. Linkerd is designed with a minimalist proxy, resulting in significant performance advantages. Studies indicate that Linkerd operates with lower latency overhead when compared to Istio, benefiting latency-sensitive applications where every microsecond counts.

The use of Envoy in Istio is a critical differentiator, as Envoy can support extensive plugin functionalities and complex routing configurations. However, this extensibility comes at the cost of higher resource usage, which may affect applications running in resource-constrained environments or require careful tuning to optimize performance.

Another lightweight option is Consul Connect, which benefits from its integration with the existing Consul infrastructure, enabling service mesh functionalities with comparatively lower complexity and overhead.

To illustrate the resource efficiency differences, consider a Kubernetes environment benchmark evaluating proxy memory usage per service instance. Linkerd's efficient memory utilization enhances its suitability for environments with limited resources, while Istio offers broader capabilities at the expense of higher consumption:

| Service Mesh | Memory per Proxy Instance |
| --- | --- |
| Linkerd | 20MB |
| Istio (with Envoy) | 50-120MB |

**Feature Set and Customizability:** The delineation of features across service meshes varies significantly, affecting how they can be molded to meet specific business needs. Istio presents a more exhaustive feature set, including rich policy management, fine-grained traffic control, and hybrid deployment support, where organizations can manage a blend of cloud-based and on-premises services. Here's an example of a sophisticated routing rule in Istio enabling the use of weighted load balancing:

```yaml
apiVersion: networking.istio.io/v1beta1
kind: VirtualService
metadata:
  name: myapp
spec:
  hosts:
  - "myapp.example.com"
  http:
  - route:
    - destination:
        host: myapp-v1
      weight: 80
    - destination:
        host: myapp-v2
      weight: 20
```

In comparison, Linkerd focuses on core utility, notably simplifying security, traffic management, and observability. The standard practices of mutual TLS, fault tolerance, and simple traffic splits make Linkerd appealing for teams seeking to enhance the resilience and security of their services without an overwhelming feature overload.

Consul Connect is noted for its first-class service discovery and network partition handling, catering well to scenarios involving dynamic and large-scale service deployments, especially when relied upon in heterogeneous environments involving other components of the HashiCorp stack.

AWS App Mesh, meanwhile, integrates effortlessly with AWS services, making it an appealing option for organizations fully invested in the AWS ecosystem, optimizing cross-service communication under its managed suite of tools.

**Community and Support:** The decision to implement a service mesh often extends beyond technical considerations to include the strength and inclusivity of its community and support ecosystem. Linkerd is backed by a vibrant and active community with an emphasis on inclusivity and supportiveness. The project's commitment to transparency and accessibility reflects in its documentation and community engagements, assisting users at all skill levels in leveraging and contributing to the platform.

Istio, co-developed by Google, IBM, and Lyft, receives significant contributions from a broad range of organizations, offering an extensive user base and a wealth of resources in terms of community support and educational materials. AWS App Mesh benefits from Amazon's robust support systems and documentation tailored to AWS users, providing streamlined support for customers already vested in AWS services.

Consul Connect's community aligns itself closely with HashiCorp, benefiting from their proven track record in infrastructure management and consistent improvements driven by enterprise requirements.

In summary, the selection of a service mesh like Linkerd, Istio, Consul Connect, or AWS App Mesh should be a strategic decision based on specific deployment scenarios, operational goals, and existing ecosystem infrastructure. The minimalist and performant architecture of Linkerd appeals to teams seeking straightforward service mesh solutions, while Istio's comprehensive features cater to enterprises requiring complex policy configurations. Consul Connect provides a unique synergy with existing Consul environments, and AWS App Mesh offers an integrated experience for users entrenched in AWS's ecosystem. This rich diversity in options ensures that organizations can select a service mesh most aligned with their strategic objectives, potential constraints, and future growth plans.

## 1.4 Core Components of Linkerd

Linkerd is distinguished by its streamlined architecture, designed to enhance the reliability, security, and performance of microservices communications in cloud-native environments. It achieves this through a carefully crafted set of core components that work harmoniously together. This section provides an in-depth exploration of these integral components, drawing connections to their functional roles and highlighting how they collectively fulfill the objectives of a modern service mesh.

The architecture of Linkerd is typically bifurcated into two primary planes — the control plane and the data plane, each comprising different components that facilitate operational capabilities and manage data flows. Understanding these components provides insight into how Linkerd implements service mesh functionality efficiently.

**Control Plane Components:**

- **Control Plane:** At the heart of Linkerd's control plane are several components that perform foundational management functions for the mesh. These include the API server, which acts as a gateway for configuring and managing the mesh, and various controllers responsible for distributing routing configurations and policies to the data plane proxies. The control plane is implemented as a collection of microservices themselves, running typically within a Kubernetes cluster.

- **Destination:** This component is tasked with service discovery and session initiation within the mesh. It resolves the destinations for traffic requests, enabling dynamic routing and ensuring that requests reach the correct recipient services. It leverages Kubernetes' service discovery APIs to get the list of endpoints for the services, maintaining up-to-date mappings to distribute to proxies in real time.

```
apiVersion: v1
kind: Service
metadata:
  name: myapp
  labels:
    app: myapp
spec:
  ports:
  - port: 80
    targetPort: 8080
```

- **Identity:** This component manages service-to-service identity and provides cryptographic credentials for mutual TLS (mTLS). It issues, rotates, and manages TLS certificates, ensuring secure and authenticated communications between services within the mesh. The Identity service relies on Kubernetes' role-based access control (RBAC) to ensure that only authorized services receive certificates.

**Data Plane Components:**

- **Linkerd Proxy:** Each instance of a service within the cluster runs a Linkerd proxy as a sidecar. The proxy intercepts incoming and outgoing requests, providing functionalities such as mTLS-enabled secure communication, transparent retries, and adaptive routing. Implemented in Rust, it ensures lightweight operation with minimal latency impact, enabling high performance even in resource-constrained environments.

- **Error Handling and Retries:** The Linkerd proxy offers intelligent retry logic and error handling capabilities, automatically retrying failed requests where deemed appropriate. This functionality preserves service resilience and continuity, efficiently managing transient faults.

```
apiVersion: linkerd.io/v1
kind: ServiceProfile
metadata:
  name: myservice.default.svc.cluster.local
spec:
  retries:
    retryable:
      - condition: 5xx
        isRetryable: true
        minTimeout: 1s
        maxTimeout: 5s
        retries: 3
```

In the configuration example above, failed requests that fall within the '5xx' range are automatically retried up to three times with escalating timeouts to account for transient errors.

**Observability Toolset:**

- **Metrics Collection:** Linkerd provides deep observability through automatic metrics collection at each proxy. Metrics such as latency, request volume, and request success rate are gathered for every service communication. These are exposed in a format compatible with Prometheus, enabling integration with existing monitoring solutions.

- **Traffic Visualization:** Linkerd offers visualization tools like the CLI and Grafana dashboards that help in inspecting service dependencies and monitoring health in real time. These tools support operators in gaining instant insights into the performance and reliability of the service mesh, aiding in timely troubleshooting and optimization efforts.

```
linkerd stat deploy
```

Using the 'linkerd stat' command, users can extract and display service metrics directly, offering a quick overview of service health.

**Security Mechanisms:**

- **Mutual TLS (mTLS):** Security is a priority in Linkerd, which automatically creates secure communication channels within the mesh via a robust mTLS framework. This framework encrypts all service-to-service traffic and facilitates mutual authentication between communicating entities.

- **Zero Trust Networking:** Linkerd enforces a zero-trust security model, enabling service access control based on authenticated identities rather than network topologies. This model is critical in mitigating risks associated with perimeter breaches, ensuring a secure inter-service trust boundary.

```
apiVersion: policy.linkerd.io/v1beta1
kind: ServerAuthorization
metadata:
  name: myservice-authorization
spec:
  server:
    name: myservice
  authorizedPrincipals:
  - "client.service-account.default.identity.linkerd.cluster.local"
```

The mTLS policy above restricts access to 'myservice' to only those defined by the specified principal, inherently following zero-trust principles.

Linkerd's suite of core components is crafted to simplify and secure service-to-service communications in microservice architectures. By providing high performance alongside ease of deployment, Linkerd enhances resilience, observability, and the security posture of applications. These capabilities are delivered without imposing significant operational overhead, embodying Linkerd's mission to refine and streamline service mesh applications for developers and operators alike.

The collective synergy of Linkerd's components allows operators to confidently construct a secure and observable microservices ecosystem. Its lightweight nature, built upon a thoughtful combination of operationally crucial features, makes it an increasingly compelling choice for organizations aiming to solidify their cloud-native environments without unwarranted complexity. Understanding these core components fortifies an operator's ability to leverage Linkerd effectively, driving innovation while maintaining service integrity and operational efficiency.

## 1.5 History and Development of Linkerd

Linkerd holds the distinction of being one of the first open-source projects to introduce the concept of a service mesh to the world of microservices and cloud-native architectures. Its journey from inception to prominence is characterized by innovation, community-driven development, and a continuous emphasis on simplicity and performance. This section provides a comprehensive exploration of Linkerd's history and development, including its technical evolution, community impact, and the role it plays within the service mesh ecosystem.

The inception of Linkerd can be traced back to 2016, when Buoyant, a company specializing in cloud-native application solutions, released it as an open-source project. The introduction of Linkerd marked a pivotal moment in addressing the challenges of inter-service communication in distributed systems, specifically aiming to solve issues related to observability, reliability, and security.

The early design of Linkerd was inspired by concepts found in network management proxies and load balancers but adapted to meet the scalable needs of microservices. Built initially on the Java-based Netty networking library and the Twitter Finagle library, Linkerd 1.x focused on robustness and operational tools critical to large-scale cloud deployments. This initial version of Linkerd offered many of the core functionalities that would define the notion of a service mesh, such as dynamic routing, service discovery, tracing, and metrics collection.

In its formative years, Linkerd quickly attracted contributions from a burgeoning community of developers who sought to enhance microservices management tools. This growing interest laid the groundwork for Linkerd to become a key project within the Cloud Native Computing Foundation (CNCF), which it joined as an incubating project in early 2017, further solidifying its relevance in cloud-native environments.

The architectural evolution of Linkerd took a significant turn in 2018 with the introduction of Linkerd 2.0. This version marked a radical departure from earlier efforts, as it was completely rewritten in Rust and Go to prioritize performance, security, and ease of use, aligning with the CNCF's philosophy of highly performant and flexible cloud-native solutions. This architectural shift reduced the complexity associated with adopting a service mesh and provided operators with a much simpler installation and operational experience.

Linkerd 2.0 also embraced the burgeoning Kubernetes ecosystem, aligning its architecture with Kubernetes' native concepts, which enhanced its compatibility and integration capabilities. This strategic alignment allowed Linkerd to leverage Kubernetes' robust service discovery, namespace, and deployment mechanisms, which significantly simplified the control plane operations.

A standout feature introduced in Linkerd 2.0 was its lightweight Rust-based proxy. This choice of language and architecture dramatically improved the efficiency and performance over the Java-based proxy used in Linkerd 1.x. The use of Rust allowed Linkerd to achieve memory safety without the overhead of a garbage collector, which is particularly advantageous in reducing latency in high-throughput environments.

Community involvement and the open-source ethos fundamentally shape Linkerd's development. With an active and engaged community, Linkerd regularly evolves to incorporate new features and improvements derived from real-world use cases. The project benefits from contributions that enhance its scope, functionality, and adaptability.

Linkerd's commitment to community engagement is evident through regular releases, comprehensive documentation, and active participation in cloud-native symposiums and conferences. This engagement facilitates rich feedback loops between end-users and developers, ensuring that Linkerd continuously evolves to meet emerging needs in distributed computing.

Several seminal versions and enhancements have marked Linkerd's progress, each advancing the capabilities and accessibility of the service mesh. Notable releases include:

- **Linkerd 2.1:** Introduced automatic mTLS for security without configuration overhead, democratizing secure service communication across all mesh participants.

- **Linkerd 2.3:** Brought significant observability improvements, including a tap feature for real-time introspection of service communication, allowing for immediate operational insights.

  ```
  linkerd tap deploy/myapp
  ```

  By executing the linkerd tap command, operators can visually inspect traffic in real time, gaining invaluable insights for debugging and optimizing service interactions.

- **Linkerd 2.7:** Expanded its capabilities with extensions like the multi-cluster feature, allowing Linkerd to manage services across multiple Kubernetes clusters seamlessly.

  ```
  apiVersion: linkerd.io/v1alpha1
  kind: Link
  metadata:
    name: west-cluster
    namespace: linkerd-multicluster
  spec:
    targetClusterName: west-cluster
    targetClusterDomains:
    - "example.west.cluster"
  ```

  This configuration exemplifies how Linkerd facilitates cross-cluster setup, presenting users with the ability to link disparate environments under a unified mesh framework.

- **Linkerd 2.10 and Beyond:** Continued the trajectory with improvements in proxy performance, dashboard enhancements, and further integration with CNCF projects, such as the Service Mesh Interface (SMI), which promotes interoperability across different service meshes.

As Linkerd matured, its influence expanded, with organizations of varying sizes and industries recognizing its utility. Enterprises have leveraged Linkerd to enhance service reliability, increase security postures, and deepen observability—all while maintaining a commitment to a straightforward and performant infrastructure layer.

Linkerd's role within the broader context of service meshes has also spurred significant dialogue around patterns and best practices in managing microservices at scale. By providing a template for efficient cloud-native networking, Linkerd has inspired both competitive and complementary projects alike, iterating on aspects of service mesh technology.

The story of Linkerd illustrates a broader narrative within the field of cloud-native transformations: a focus on community-driven, open-source innovation leading to substantial shifts in how burgeoning architectures are managed and optimized. Its ongoing evolution promises to keep pace with the trends shaping distributed application delivery, with aims for further integration, adaptability, and community-driven growth defining its path forward.

Linkerd has not only pioneered service mesh principles but remains at the forefront of shaping modern application networking practices. Its history and development reflect a steadfast commitment to simplicity, performance, and empowerment of users through robust, easy-to-deploy solutions fostered within an engaged community ecosystem.

# Chapter 2

# Architecture of Linkerd

Linkerd's architecture is designed to manage service-to-service communication efficiently by leveraging a combination of control and data plane components. The control plane oversees configurations and policies, while the data plane, consisting of lightweight proxies, handles the actual traffic between services. This chapter delves into the core architectural components of Linkerd, including the sidecar pattern, service discovery mechanisms, and routing capabilities. Additionally, it explores configuration nuances, scalability considerations, and the robustness that ensures fault tolerance within a service mesh deployment. Through this examination, the architecture of Linkerd is unpacked to highlight how it balances simplicity with powerful functionality.

## 2.1 Linkerd Control Plane

The Linkerd control plane is a vital component in managing traffic and ensuring the policies are effectively implemented across a service mesh. It operates as the brain of the Linkerd architecture, overseeing the configurations and maintaining coherence among the distributed services by interacting with the data plane's proxies. This section delves into its structure, functionality, and role in service mesh governance, along with code examples illustrating its operation and customization.

**Core Components of the Linkerd Control Plane**

Linkerd's control plane is composed of several microservices, each serving a dedicated purpose within its scope of mesh management. The core components include:

- Controller: Acts as the control server, coordinating the various services.
- Web: Provides a user interface through which operators can view the status of the mesh.
- Destination: Handles service discovery, enabling efficient service-to-service communication.
- Identity: Performs secure certification of the services within the mesh.
- Proxy Injector: Facilitates the injection of the Linkerd proxy sidecar into Kubernetes pods.
- Multicluster: Manages services that span across multiple clusters.

These components work together to ensure that the control plane can effectively manage the activities of all associated data plane entities, implementing traffic policies, and ensuring integrity and security within the service mesh.

**Traffic Management and Policy Enforcement**

The control plane plays a key role in abstracting away complexities of traffic management. It uses the service discovery component to map service names to actual network locations within the mesh. This operation is critical in achieving seamless communication, where requests are dynamically routed based on the service registry maintained by the control plane.

The following illustrates how service discovery is efficiently executed using JSON output from the Destination component:

## 2.1. LINKERD CONTROL PLANE

```
{
  "name": "httpbin.default.svc.cluster.local",
  "namespace": "default",
  "addresses": [
    {
      "ip": "10.0.75.2",
      "port": 80
    }
  ],
  "protocol": "http",
  "labels": {}
}
```

Such information is pivotal to Linkerd proxies in mapping requests to the correct service endpoints, enabled by the seamless integration facilitated by the control plane.

In terms of policy enforcement, the control plane implements and manages service policies using various configuration resources like Authorization policies and TrafficSplit controls. These configurations are imperative for defining which services can communicate and how traffic is distributed.

```
kind: TrafficSplit
apiVersion: split.smi-spec.io/v1alpha1
metadata:
  name: example-split
  namespace: default
spec:
  service: backend
  backends:
  - service: backend-v1
    weight: 80
  - service: backend-v2
    weight: 20
```

In the YAML configuration above, TrafficSplit allows operators to designate how incoming connections to the 'backend' service are distributed among different versions. Through such configurations, the control plane orchestrates traffic flows and adaptations dynamically, all while maintaining alignment with strategic service priorities.

**Security and Identity Management**

One of the distinguishing features of Linkerd's control plane is its ability to manage and enforce end-to-end encryption via mutual TLS (mTLS). The Identity service automates key and certificate issuance for the proxies, leveraging Kubernetes secrets and cert-manager integrations to maintain secure communications.

The automatic lifecycle management of certificates by the Identity service reduces operational overhead and ensures that all communications within the mesh are secured. Each service within the mesh is assigned a service identity, which is validated by the Identity component to facilitate mTLS encryption.

The mTLS setup can be illustrated through Helm configuration snippets that are used to customize certificate issuance and management:

```
linkerdIdentity:
  issuer:
    scheme: kubernetes.io/tls
    crtExpiry: 24h
```

This snippet specifies a Kubernetes-managed certificate issuer and configures the expiry time for the certificates to ensure regular renewal and secured operations.

**Proxy Injection via Webhooks**

The Proxy Injector is a critical mechanism within the Linkerd control plane that automates the sidecar injection process. This component operates as a dynamic admission webhook in Kubernetes, modifying pod specifications to include the Linkerd proxy sidecar containers at the time of their creation.

The webhook approach streamlines the injection process, allowing Linkerd to seamlessly integrate into existing services and maintain consistency across deployments. Aside from providing automation, this also ensures that any new or updated services are immediately granted the benefits of the service mesh without manual interventions.

**Monitoring and Visibility**

Another pivotal function of the control plane is to offer robust monitoring and visibility into mesh operations. The Web component is central to this, translating control plane telemetry into a human-readable format that operators can utilize for insights.

Telemetry data collected can be displayed in real-time dashboards or used for retrospective analysis, guiding service optimizations and operational improvements. Grafana and Prometheus integrations serve as common elements utilized for monitoring purposes, offering a framework through which metrics and alerts can be effectively configured. Example Prometheus queries might include:

```
sum(rate(linkerd_http_requests_total{direction="inbound"}[5m]))
```

This query calculates the inbound HTTP requests rate, aiding in usage pattern analysis and capacity planning.

**Multicluster Management**

Linkerd extends its control plane capabilities through the Multicluster component for applications that span multiple clusters. This component coordinates traffic between disparate environments, enabling them as if part of a single cohesive mesh.

Cross-cluster communication employs shared trust domains, requiring coordinated identity management and service discovery extensions. This capability is essential for enterprises that require robust cross-environment networking underpinned by security and reliability.

Each of these features effectively illustrates the extensive capabilities of the Linkerd control plane. The synergy between its components empowers operators to achieve the dual goals of operational simplicity and robust functionality.

## 2.2 Linkerd Data Plane

The Linkerd data plane forms the execution engine of the service mesh, responsible for managing the real-time flow of traffic between microservices. Unlike the control plane, which is about orchestration and overall system management, the data plane functions at the operational level, instilling control over the traffic that traverses the service mesh. This section elaborates on the intricacies of the Linkerd data plane, detailing its structural elements, operational algorithms, and the pivotal role it plays in service communication. The discussion is enriched with coding examples to demonstrate its mechanisms and operational parameters.

**Architecture and Components of the Data Plane**

At its core, the Linkerd data plane comprises a network of lightweight proxies deployed as sidecars alongside service instances within Kubernetes pods. These proxies, crafted in the Rust programming language, are renowned for their efficiency and minimal overhead. The default Linkerd proxy is responsible for service discovery, service-to-service communication, load balancing, and telemetry collection, implementing policies defined by the control plane.

Each Linkerd proxy is injected into a pod where it intercepts both inbound and outbound traffic. The interaction sequence between these proxies and the overall service mesh fabric is paramount in delivering resilient and reliable service communication.

**Traffic Management**

Traffic management within the data plane is multifaceted, involving processes such as load balancing, retry policies, and failure recovery.

- **Load Balancing**: Each proxy contains a highly efficient load balancer that manages the selection of service endpoints based on load and performance metrics. The load balancer dynamically updates its logic based on real-time telemetry, ensuring optimal request distribution across healthy service instances. The algorithm operates on relative metrics, automatically rerouting traffic from degraded endpoints.

```
fn endpoint_selection(endpoints: Vec<Endpoint>) -> Endpoint {
    endpoints.iter().min_by_key(|e| e.latency).unwrap().clone()
}
```

In the Rust snippet above, endpoints are iterated over to select the one with the lowest latency, demonstrating a simplistic approach to load balancing logic within the proxy.

- **Retry Policies and Failure Recovery**: Retry logic is a key component of resilient communication in the data plane. The proxies execute retry policies configured by the control plane, enabling them to automatically handle transient failures. The retries are instrumented intelligently, ensuring they do not overload systems or contribute to cascading failures.

```
tracing:
  retry_budget:
    retry_ratio: 0.2
    min_retries_per_second: 10
```

The YAML snippet demonstrates how retry budgets are configured, constraining retries to prevent overuse and further failure propagation.

**Security via mTLS**

A core competency of the Linkerd data plane is its native support for end-to-end encryption using mutual TLS (mTLS). Each proxy is equipped to perform encryption and decryption tasks, assuring secure service-to-service communication.

The Linkerd data plane enforces mTLS by generating unique identity credentials for each service proxy. These credentials are securely exchanged, enabling mTLS handshakes that verify the identity and authenticity of communicating services.

The automated establishment of secure channels ensures all traffic within the mesh is protected against unauthorized access and potential data breaches. Encryption policies are managed transparently, reducing the operational burden related to manual key management processes.

```
linkerd viz install | kubectl apply -f -
```

The above command illustrates how to enable monitoring of mTLS state using Linkerd's visualization tools, helping operators ensure compliance with security policies.

**Telemetry Collection**

Telemetry plays a vital role in Linkerd's data plane, providing metrics crucial for operational insights and performance tuning. The proxies are tasked with collecting telemetry data and forwarding it to the control plane for aggregation.

Out-of-the-box, Linkerd proxies gather statistics regarding:

- Request counts and latencies,
- Success and error rates,
- mTLS handshake success.

These metrics culminate in real-time dashboards, facilitating operational visibility and efficient troubleshooting. Linkerd's integration with Prometheus is a vital element of its telemetry infrastructure, enabling it to expose metrics through well-defined endpoints that Prometheus scrapes.

```
rate(request_total{status!="200"}[5m])
```

This Prometheus query yields the error rate over a five-minute window, allowing operators to focus on troubleshooting any spikes in the service failure rates.

**Service Discovery and Routing**

Service discovery within the data plane relies heavily on the control plane's real-time data feed, enabling intelligent routing decisions. Proxies utilize service identity caches maintained by the control plane to rapidly locate and connect with the correct service instances.

The data plane implements consistent hashing and other strategies to route traffic efficiently, optimizing request paths and ensuring service availability. Linkerd facilitates service discovery through:

- Dynamic peer lists informed by the Destination control plane service,
- Traffic splits and failovers for redundancy.

Such mechanisms ensure that traffic is always flowing through the optimal path, with reduced latency and improved user experiences.

**Conclusion of Review**

A comprehensive exploration of Linkerd's data plane highlights its fundamental attributes of security, efficiency, and resilience. While the data plane operates under the policies and instructions issued by the control plane, its autonomous operation is crucial to the reliable functioning of the service mesh. Every component—from traffic management to telemetry collection—plays a strategic role in delivering on Linkerd's promise of seamless service communication and observability.

As Linkerd continues to evolve, its data plane remains a crucial frontier for innovation in microservices networking, blending sophisticated protocols with practical control mechanisms to meet the demands of modern cloud-native environments. "'

**Note**: The image 'linkerd-data-plane-architecture.png' was reported as missing. Ensure this file exists in the specified path or update the path if necessary.

## 2.3 Sidecar Pattern in Linkerd

The sidecar pattern is a fundamental architectural practice in microservices architecture, where auxiliary functions of a service are abstracted into companion components known as "sidecars." In the context of Linkerd, the sidecar pattern is crucial as it underpins the service mesh architecture, enhancing modularity, maintainability, and scalability. This section delineates the sidecar pattern's role within Linkerd, underscored by its contribution to seamless integration, observability, decentralized control, and enhanced security in a microservices ecosystem.

**Understanding the Sidecar Pattern**

The sidecar pattern involves deploying a secondary container, or "sidecar," alongside the primary service container in the same pod. This compartmentalization enables a clear separation of concerns, enhancing manageability and deployment flexibility by delineating auxiliary tasks from the core service functionality.

In Linkerd's architecture, each service instance is paired with a proxy sidecar. This proxy acts as an intermediary for all incoming and outgoing traffic to the service, executing decision-making and transformation tasks based on telemetry, service discovery, and security policies dictated by the control plane.

**Advantages of the Sidecar Pattern**

The incorporation of the sidecar pattern within Linkerd offers several distinct advantages that significantly enhance the service mesh functionality:

- API Gateway Capacities: The proxy sidecar extends expanded API management capabilities, effortlessly implementing standards for API traffic routing and direct orchestration of service interactions.

- Improved Observability: By gathering telemetry at the mesh's edges, sidecars facilitate robust logging, metrics collection, and monitoring, independent of the service's internal code.

- Decoupled Development and Maintenance: Service developers can focus intently on business logic, while independent teams manage sidecar functionality, ushering in specialist interventions and updates.

- Cross-cutting Concerns Management: Concerns like security, logging, and communication occur across service boundaries and can be controlled consistently outside of the service's business logic.

The sidecar pattern's implementation in Linkerd is instrumental for consistent, reliable, and scalable service interactions, bridging diverse aspects of service management into an integrated, functioning whole.

**Operational Mechanics**

The sidecar pattern enables the successful execution of a range of critical tasks within the service mesh. These include:

- Traffic Interception: All communication to and from a service instance is intercepted by the proxy sidecar. This allows for enhanced visibility into network traffic and provides a direct path for implementing custom logic for request handling.

```
func proxyHandler(req *http.Request) (*http.Response, error) {
    // Apply custom logic
    modifiedReq := augmentRequest(req)

    // Forward to the actual service
    return http.DefaultClient.Do(modifiedReq)
}
```

This Go function exemplifies a basic framework for how a sidecar might intercept and modify HTTP requests, ultimately forwarding them to the main service component.

- Dynamic Configuration: The sidecar can dynamically adjust configurations and behaviors based on telemetry inputs and policies set by the control plane, adapting to real-time changes in the network environment.

## 2.3. SIDECAR PATTERN IN LINKERD

- Security Management: **As all traffic is funneled through the sidecar, mTLS encryption, authentication, and authorization processes are centralized, with identities and certificates managed securely.**

```
apiVersion: v1
kind: ConfigMap
metadata:
  name: linkerd-config
data:
  identity-issuer.tls.crtPEM: |
    -----BEGIN CERTIFICATE-----
    MIIBIjC...
    -----END CERTIFICATE-----
  identity-issuer.tls.keyPEM: |
    -----BEGIN RSA PRIVATE KEY-----
    MIIEpAIB...
    -----END RSA PRIVATE KEY-----
```

The ConfigMap in this snippet points to a secure management of certificates, making TLS setups manageable and repeatable across environments.

- Fault Injection: **The ability to simulate faults such as delays or errors within the sidecar allows for comprehensive testing of service resilience, aiding in proactive identification and rectification of potential weaknesses.**

## Deployment Scenarios and Challenges

Deploying sidecars entails certain considerations specific to the complexity and nature of the application services involved:

- Resource Management: **Although resource overhead is minimal, the added container of the sidecar increases the resource allocation footprint per pod, requiring meticulous resource management and capacity planning.**

- Deployment Strategies: **Effective roll-out strategies such as canary deployments should be adopted to manage gradual roll-outs of sidecars to ensure seamless integration with the existing application infrastructure.**

- Versioning and Compatibility: **As sidecars are distributed systems components, compatibility with the service lifecycle, ver-**

sioning, and orchestrated upgrades need precise choreography to sustain overall service reliability.

The key lies in harmonizing operations across these axes to assure the sidecar's successful incorporation into the service network.

**Security Implications**

From a security standpoint, the sidecar pattern is instrumental to enforcing zero-trust networking paradigms within Linkerd. By implementing mTLS, the proxy ensures that data in transit remains confidential and authentic:

- Identity Verification: Each sidecar is provisioned a unique identity, authenticated by the control plane, to represent its associated service reliably.

- Access Control Policies: Fine-grained policies defined at the control plane are executed by sidecars, dynamically dictating who or what is permitted to access specific services.

- Compliance and Auditing: The isolation of traffic handling functions to sidecars allows comprehensive logging and auditing capabilities, essential for maintaining compliance in certain regulatory environments.

```
SELECT timestamp, source_ip, destination_ip, status
FROM traffic_logs
WHERE status != "200"
```

This SQL query could represent the process of auditing traffic logs for irregularities, leveraging sidecar-captured data to provide insight.

**Conclusion of Use and Future Implications**

The sidecar pattern's integration into Linkerd's architecture is a testament to the pattern's capability in managing and enhancing microservices architectures. As microservices continue to evolve, the sidecar pattern ensures that auxiliary services can scale organically and adapt to technological innovations without necessitating code refactoring in the core application.

The maturity of the sidecar pattern points towards future scenarios where machine-learning models and context-based adaptations run natively within the sidecar, thus realizing advanced service interaction frameworks characterized by autonomy and intelligence.

Through continuous improvements, especially in areas of automation and resilience, the sidecar pattern remains steadfast in its journey to redefine modern application networking through seamless service coordination and maximized operational efficiencies.

## 2.4 Service Discovery and Routing

Service discovery and routing are critical facets of any microservices architecture, including service meshes like Linkerd. They ensure that requests are correctly directed to available instances of services, thereby maintaining the fluidity and resilience of applications distributed across clustered environments. In Linkerd, these functionalities are architected to provide scalability, failover, and dynamic load distribution, offering a seamless operation underpinning microservice interactions. This section examines the mechanisms of service discovery and routing within Linkerd, supported by coding examples and analysis that illustrate their implementation and efficacy.

### Service Discovery Mechanisms

Service discovery in a service mesh involves automatically identifying available service instances within a network. Linkerd accomplishes this through its Destination controller, part of the control plane, which collects endpoint information and pushes updates to the data plane proxies whenever the network topology changes.

The diagram above visualizes how service discovery feeds information into the proxies, highlighting the dynamic and real-time nature of service awareness within the mesh.

- **Automatic Registration**: As services start, they automatically register with Linkerd's control plane via Kubernetes' native DNS capabilities, wherein their endpoints are cataloged.

- **Dynamic Resolution**: The Destination controller supplies the proxy sidecars with updated service lists, leveraging Kubernetes DNS and distributed systems processes to ensure that proxies receive the latest service state data.

- **Real-time Updates**: Whenever there are changes, such as scaling operations, the control plane distributes these updates to maintain consistent state across all proxies in the mesh.

```
type Endpoints struct {
    // Representation of available endpoints
    Ip string
    Port int
}

func resolveService(svc string) []Endpoints {
    // Logic for service discovery resolution
    endpoints := queryDns(svc)
    return endpoints
}
```

This Go code snippet demonstrates a simplified function to resolve a service name to its endpoints, leveraging DNS queries which is akin to the process normalized by Linkerd for proxy awareness.

### Routing Strategy and Mechanisms

Service routing in Linkerd helps direct requests from a source to the desired endpoint service, established through a set of sophisticated, policy-driven algorithms.

- **Load Balancing**: Within each proxy, load balancing decisions are dynamically adjusted based on live telemetry, adhering to connection pooling and latency improvement strategies. This enables traffic distribution to be fluid and reflective of real-time service state.

- **Traffic Splitting**: Linkerd's control plane empowers the specification of traffic splits, useful in rollouts such as canary deployments or versioning, enabling gradual exposure of features.

```
kind: TrafficSplit
apiVersion: split.smi-spec.io/v1alpha3
```

## 2.4. SERVICE DISCOVERY AND ROUTING

```
metadata:
  name: example-traffic-split
  namespace: default
spec:
  service: web-page
  backends:
  - service: web-v1
    weight: 90
  - service: web-v2
    weight: 10
```

In this YAML configuration, a TrafficSplit object is defined to distribute 90% of traffic to web-v1 and 10% to web-v2, illustrating control over service routing and version management.

- **Failover Policies**: Linkerd integrates health checks and failover policies, directing traffic away from non-responsive hosts. Failure detections trigger automatic rerouting to ensure service continuity and user satisfaction.

```
fn handle_request(request: HttpRequest) -> HttpResponse {
    match is_healthy(&request.destination()) {
        true => forward_to_service(&request),
        false => redirect_to_backup()
    }
}
```

The Rust snippet encapsulates a rudimentary concept of handling request rerouting within a sidecar if health checks indicate a failure, ensuring only healthy services handle production traffic.

### Enhancements and Observability

Service routing goes hand-in-hand with observability in Linkerd ensuring that the real-time state of the service mesh is always visible to operators:

- **Telemetry and Metrics Collection**: By aggregating request metrics such as latencies, success rates, and load distribution statistics, Linkerd offers a pervasive view into service interactions, facilitating predictive scaling and incidence response.

```
rate(http_request_duration_seconds_bucket[5m])
```

This query demonstrates the aggregate metrics for request durations over a 5-minute period, which are essential in assessing service latency trends.

- **Tracing Capabilities**: Linkerd also supports tracing to connect together the life span of a request across service boundaries, offering insights into dependencies and potential latency bottlenecks.
- **Service Dashboards**: With integrations like Grafana, visual dashboards are constructed enabling real-time monitoring surfaces for detailed operational schematics.

## Security Implications of Service Discovery and Routing

The paradigms of service discovery and routing are tightly aligned with security constructs; Linkerd ensures all communications are in compliance with secure practices.

- **Secure Channel Establishment**: All service communications conform to mTLS guidelines, with every interaction authenticated and encrypted, ensuring both data integrity and privacy.
- **Role-based Access and Policy Enforcement**: Routing decisions in Linkerd are policy-intensified, requiring compliance with role-based access governance laid out by the control plane.

Addressing such high levels of security allows organizations to mitigate threats and enforce stringent access controls, maintaining robustness in service communications.

## Conclusion of Mechanistic Review

Exploring Linkerd's service discovery and routing mechanisms reflects the intelligent design choices that sustain high availability, fault tolerance, and operability of applications within the service mesh. With comprehensive linkage across real-time feeds, intelligent routing, and observability frameworks, Linkerd cements its place as a seamless middleware, not only accommodating but enhancing microservices paradigms.

The continual evolution of service discovery and routing processes will continue to adapt alongside shifting technological trends, ensuring they remain at the forefront of network management strategies. Incorporating deeper machine learning insights or AI-driven adaptive algorithms could potentially refine Linkerd's routing capabilities even further, offering even more efficacious means to fine-tune the performance and reliability of service communications in cloud-native ecosystems.

## 2.5 Configuration and Customization

Configuration and customization lie at the heart of adapting Linkerd to meet the specific needs of diverse environments and use-cases. The architecture of Linkerd is inherently flexible, allowing operators to fine-tune various components and their interactions in a service mesh. This section elucidates the processes and options available for configuring and customizing Linkerd, detailing components' settings and their practical implications. Additionally, it presents best practices for tailoring Linkerd deployments to align with organizational and operational goals.

### Installation and Initial Configuration

The journey of configuring Linkerd begins with its installation, tailored to meet specific infrastructure requirements. Linkerd can be deployed using either the CLI-based linkerd install command or Helm charts, both offering a breadth of parameters to specify.

- **CLI Installation**: The Linkerd CLI is a straightforward way to install and customize a basic Linkerd configuration. The following command outlines a primary installation:

```
linkerd install --ha | kubectl apply -f -
```

The $-ha$ flag in the CLI specifies a high-availability setup, configuring the control plane components for redundancy, a useful setting for production-grade deployments.

- **Helm Charts**: Helm offers the flexibility of managing complex Linkerd configurations, which can be captured within values files. A typical values file might look like this:

```
global:
  identityTrustDomain: "cluster.local"
  disableExternalProfiles: false

controller:
  replicas: 3

identity:
  issuer:
    crtExpiry: 86400s
```

In this configuration, high-availability for the control plane through three replicas and issuer certificate configurations are specified, showcasing Helm's comprehensive approach to managing installations with repeatable configurations.

**Component Configuration**

Linkerd's architecture permits fine-grained adjustments and optimizations of its control and data plane components.

- **Proxy Customization**: Proxies, central to the data plane, can be finely tuned to optimize resource utilization and enhance performance.

    - **Resource Management**: Configuring the sidecar proxy's CPU and memory limits ensures it uses resources proportionately, reducing overhead while maximizing throughput.

    ```
    resources:
      requests:
        cpu: "100m"
        memory: "64Mi"
      limits:
        cpu: "500m"
        memory: "256Mi"
    ```

    Specifying the resource requests and limits for proxy containers can alleviate bottlenecks from resource contention, effectively balancing service performance with available hardware constraints.

    - **Timeout and Retries**: Response timeout and retry policies within proxies can also be tuned:

    ```
    linkerd.io/proxy:
      config: |
        inbound:
    ```

## 2.5. CONFIGURATION AND CUSTOMIZATION

```
    timeout: 5s
    retries: 3
```

Configurations like these dictate how proxies manage network failures, providing resilience through automatic request re-routing and maintaining seamless service interactions.

- **Control Plane Settings**: The control plane can be scaled up for higher default throughput, and its components configured for optimal performance under varying load conditions.

```
controller:
  replicaCount: 3
identity:
  issuer:
    crtExpiry: 60h
```

This example illustrates scaling up control plane integrity by increasing the number of replicas and adjusting certificate expiration to balance security with renewal costs.

**Traffic and Policy Customization**

Customizing traffic management and network policies within Linkerd allows operators to guardrail their mesh with precise control.

- **Traffic Splitting**: By dynamically distributing traffic using SMI TrafficSplit policies, teams can safely deploy new features and scale components incrementally.

```
apiVersion: split.smi-spec.io/v1alpha1
kind: TrafficSplit
metadata:
  name: canary
  namespace: metrics
spec:
  service: telemetry
  backends:
  - service: telemetry-v1
    weight: 95
  - service: telemetry-canary
    weight: 5
```

Such configuration allows operators to verify potential impacts of newly deployed instances under realistic load conditions, helping identify issues early.

- **Network Policies**: Through customized network policies, Linkerd can define the permitted communications between services:

```
kind: NetworkPolicy
apiVersion: networking.k8s.io/v1
metadata:
  name: allow-specific-sources
spec:
  podSelector:
    matchLabels:
      app: payment
  policyTypes:
  - Ingress
  ingress:
  - from:
    - podSelector:
        matchLabels:
          role: frontend
```

This policy ensures that only pods with a specific role can communicate with the payment service, creating secure zones within the service network and aligning with zero-trust security principles.

## Custom Telemetry and Observability

Fine-tuning observability settings in Linkerd involves adjusting telemetry outputs and integrating them with broader monitoring systems.

- **Prometheus Integration**: Defining custom scrape configurations enhances understanding of both network and application-level metrics which can be output to systems like Prometheus.

```
scrape_configs:
  - job_name: 'linkerd-proxy'
    static_configs:
      - targets: ['localhost:4191']
```

This configuration informs Prometheus to scrape metrics from each proxy, providing comprehensive visibility into mesh activity.

- **Dashboard Customization**: Tailoring Grafana dashboards enables focused metric visualization that aligns with given operational priorities.

Custom queries or transforms can be implemented in Grafana to

## 2.5. CONFIGURATION AND CUSTOMIZATION

feature key performance indicators, detecting anomalies or guiding strategic decisions that leverage historical data trends.

```
sum(rate(http_requests_total{job="linkerd"}[1m])) by (route)
```

By aggregating requests over routes, operational teams can track application usage patterns and uncover pivotal traffic bottlenecks early.

**Advanced Customization Scenarios**

Linkerd provides mechanisms for advanced customization to accommodate specific service demands or orchestration strategies:

- **Custom Plugins and Extensions**: Enabling external plugins or custom extensions involves creating sidecar injectors that include user-developed logic, enhancing the mesh's capabilities.

- **Integration with CI/CD Pipelines**: Configuration-driven deployments allow for continuous delivery pipelines that deploy service changes and mesh configurations cohesively, reducing deployment times and human error.

- **Automated Policy Management**: Constructs that define automated policy management dynamically adjust based on system telemetry, offering highly responsive security measures without manual oversight.

**Conclusion of Configuration Efficacy**

Through the configurations and customizations discussed, Linkerd supports a powerful framework for designing robust, detailed, and adaptable architectures in a service mesh. By providing developers and operators with concentrated avenues for precision tuning and dynamic response to network conditions, Linkerd manifests as an adaptable and resilient choice for modern microservices platforms. Future iterations may extend even deeper into machine-learning-driven optimizations, enhancing responsiveness and autonomy within complex system environments.

## 2.6 Scalability and Fault Tolerance

Scalability and fault tolerance are fundamental properties required for a service mesh, ensuring that applications can grow to accommodate increased loads while maintaining uninterrupted service. Linkerd's architecture is meticulously crafted to support seamless scalability and robust fault tolerance by leveraging distributed systems principles and container orchestration capabilities. This section delves into how these capabilities are built into Linkerd, examining core components, design patterns, and operational best practices, enriched with code examples to elucidate concepts and techniques.

**Scalability in Linkerd**

Scalability refers to the ability of a system to efficiently expand resource capabilities to handle growth in load or data volume. Linkerd inherently supports both vertical and horizontal scaling.

- **Horizontal Scaling:** This involves adding more instances to handle increased traffic, often done by scaling the number of pods that run a particular service. Linkerd's lightweight proxies allow this without significant overhead.

    ```yaml
    apiVersion: apps/v1
    kind: Deployment
    metadata:
      name: frontend
    spec:
      replicas: 10 # Scale the number of replicas to increase throughput
      template:
        metadata:
          labels:
            app: frontend
        spec:
          containers:
          - name: frontend
            image: my-frontend:latest
    ```

    The YAML snippet leverages Kubernetes Deployments to scale a frontend service. Adjusting the 'replicas' field ensures that requests are distributed among multiple instances, leading to increased throughput and service stability.

- **Vertical Scaling:** Though less common, vertical scaling can be applied to individual components such as the Linkerd con-

## 2.6. SCALABILITY AND FAULT TOLERANCE

trol plane. Optimizing resources to better handle peak loads improves performance further without adding to cluster size.

```
resources:
  limits:
    cpu: "2"
    memory: "4Gi"
  requests:
    cpu: "1"
    memory: "2Gi"
```

This snippet defines increased resource allocations for specific pods, accommodating higher computational needs during load spikes.

- **Traffic Distribution**: Load balancing across instances of a service ensures that no single instance becomes a bottleneck. Linkerd employs sophisticated load balancing algorithms within its proxies that continually optimize traffic distribution based on real-time metrics.

```
fn select_endpoint(endpoints: Vec<Endpoint>, metrics: &Metrics) -> Endpoint
{
    endpoints.iter().min_by_key(|e| metrics.load(e)).unwrap().clone()
}
```

The demonstrated function selects a service endpoint based on the current load, ensuring equitable traffic distribution and leveraging real-time data.

## Fault Tolerance Features

Fault tolerance is the capacity of a system to continue its intended operation, possibly at a reduced level, rather than failing completely, when some part of the system fails.

- **Automatic Failover**: Linkerd uses automatic failover to maintain service availability, rerouting requests to standby instances or replicas without user involvement.

```
if !isHealthy(primaryInstance) {
    routeTraffic(standbyInstance)
}
```

This Go code exemplifies a check that reroutes traffic to standby instances if the primary instance fails health checks, aiding continuity.

- **Retry and Circuit Breaking**: Linkerd proxies include preconfigured settings for retries and circuit breaking, preventing cascading failures within services.

```
retryBudget:
  retryRatio: 0.2
  minRetriesPerSec: 3
```

In such configurations, retry budgets limit the number of retries to prevent overwhelming a service, while circuit breaking quickly halts repeated failure patterns, adding resilience.

```
circuitBreaker:
  errorThresholdPercentage: 50
  slidingWindowSize: 20
```

Here, a circuit breaker configuration ensures that if errors exceed 50% within a 20-request window, new requests are halted to prevent server overload.

- **Resilience Testing**: Linkerd facilitates chaos engineering practices to test and enhance fault tolerance by intentionally introducing failures.

Leveraging the mesh's observability, operators can introduce synthetic failures to understand how the system will behave under pressure, enhancing robustness through real-world experimentation.

## Design Patterns and Best Practices

The ability to guarantee scalability and fault tolerance requires adherence to specific architectural patterns and operational practices.

- **Microservices Isolation**: Ensuring services remain isolated helps minimize the impact of a failure. Each service, encapsulated with its dedicated Linkerd proxy, forms a containment zone against fault propagation.

- **Monitoring and Alerting**: Comprehensive metrics and alert configurations are vital. By observing system behaviors and trends, remedial actions can be swiftly executed.

```
avg(rate(linkerd_http_request_duration_seconds_sum{status_code="500"}[5
    m])) by (service))
```

This Prometheus query calculates response errors, helping identify services with abnormalities, which may necessitate scale adjustments or performance optimizations.

- **Redundancy and Replication**: Critical services should always be replicated across different availability zones or nodes, ensuring logic and state are spared from single points of failure.

- **Hierarchical Routing and Failover**: Employ consistent hashing and hierarchical failover strategies to direct traffic through the most efficient path, mitigating delays or potential points of congestion.

**Advanced Scaling Techniques**

Scaling strategies can be extended using more advanced techniques suited to specific operational needs.

- **Service Scaling Policies**: Enforcing scaling policies aligned with traffic prediction tools ensures services grow and shrink in concert with load forecasts.

  ```
  kind: HorizontalPodAutoscaler
  apiVersion: autoscaling/v1
  metadata:
    name: backend-hpa
  spec:
    scaleTargetRef:
      apiVersion: apps/v1
      kind: Deployment
      name: backend
    minReplicas: 3
    maxReplicas: 15
    targetCPUUtilizationPercentage: 75
  ```

  The Horizontal Pod Autoscaler pictured above prescribes policies for adaptive scaling against CPU metrics, ensuring dynamic response to load variations.

- **Stateful Services Handling**: While Linkerd primarily caters to stateless workloads, seamlessly integrating it with stateful services through session affinity configurations optimizes request consistency.

- **Global Traffic Management**: Geographically distributed services utilize global traffic management tools routed through the mesh for latency or regulatory considerations.

**Conclusion of Synthesis**

Linkerd's scalability and fault tolerance are pivotal, enabling enterprises to meet their growth trajectories while maintaining exceptional reliability. With the architecture's built-in features and observability stack, Linkerd facilitates optimal service operations without degrading performance under high load or failing under duress. By adhering to established patterns and utilizing best practices, operators can craft a pathway for their organizations to navigate scale without sacrificing stability. Future innovations may see more AI-driven load balancing and predictive scaling capabilities, continually evolving to meet new challenges within the cloud-native space.

# Chapter 3

# Installing and Configuring Linkerd

Installing and configuring Linkerd involves several critical steps to ensure a seamless integration into a Kubernetes environment. This chapter provides a detailed guide, starting with understanding the system requirements, followed by the installation of the Linkerd CLI, and the deployment of the service mesh onto a Kubernetes cluster. It further elaborates on verifying the installation and configuring Linkerd to suit specific operational environments. The chapter also includes guidance on updating and maintaining Linkerd, ensuring that users can keep their deployments secure and up-to-date with the latest features and improvements.

## 3.1 System Requirements for Linkerd

Linkerd is a prominent service mesh that helps manage microservices by providing features such as observability, reliability, and security. To ensure seamless performance and integration within Kubernetes environments, understanding the system requirements for deploying Linkerd is crucial. These requirements encompass both hardware and software components essential to achieving optimal functionality for Linkerd. This section will cover the key elements necessary for a successful Linkerd deployment, addressing hardware prerequisites, software dependencies, and additional considerations that may impact performance and usability.

The deployment of Linkerd involves two main components: the control plane, which manages the operation of the service mesh, and the data plane, where the Linkerd proxies intercept and manage traffic between services. Understanding the resource requirements for each component is fundamental to ensuring efficient performance.

**Hardware Requirements:**

To effectively deploy Linkerd within a Kubernetes cluster, it is important to acknowledge the inherent hardware resources required for both the control plane and the data plane proxies.

**Control Plane Considerations:**

The control plane consists of various components such as the controller, web interface, Grafana for metrics visualization, and Prometheus for data collection. These components necessitate minimal resource allocation but their cumulative impact must not be underestimated. The resource allocation must account for future scalability and performance under high load:

- **CPU Requirements:** The control plane generally requires modest CPU resources. A baseline allocation of 0.5 to 1 CPU core should be sufficient for most medium-sized environments. However, environments with elevated scale demands may require more depending on the number of workload items.

- **Memory Requirements:** The memory footprint of the Linkerd control plane lies around 512 MiB to 1 GiB. Monitoring must aid in adjusting memory allocation as usage increases, ensuring that each component receives adequate memory under load.

- **Storage Requirements:** Persistent storage is not typically required for Linkerd's control plane as Prometheus, used for metrics storage, can leverage ephemeral storage or off-cluster storage solutions like a volume or PVC (PersistentVolumeClaim) per Kubernetes best practices.

## 3.1. SYSTEM REQUIREMENTS FOR LINKERD

**Data Plane Proxy Resource Needs:**

Each service instance within a Linkerd mesh is co-located with an instance of Linkerd's data plane proxy. This model augments requirements at scale:

- **CPU Allocation:** Proxies typically require less than 0.2 CPU cores but this value needs tuning based on the traffic volume and complexity of policies enforced. It is essential to monitor the CPU usage of proxies to ensure any surges in service consumption are adequately handled.

- **Memory Usage:** Generally, the memory usage scales linearly with service traffic. A starting point for the proxy's memory limit might be 50 to 100 MiB, scaling as necessary.

**Software Dependencies:**

Deployment of Linkerd also hinges on specific software prerequisites. A clear understanding of these dependencies ensures successful integration within a Kubernetes cluster.

- **Kubernetes Version Requirements:** Linkerd supports several Kubernetes versions, typically catering to the last few minor versions. At the time of writing, Linkerd supports Kubernetes version 1.19 and newer. It's pivotal to evaluate the Linkerd documentation for the support matrix that corresponds to the specific deployment period.

- **Operating System Compatibility:** The underlying nodes in the Kubernetes cluster must run an operating system compatible with both Kubernetes and Linkerd. Most common Linux distributions, such as Ubuntu, CentOS, and Alpine Linux, satisfy these requirements.

- **Command-Line Interface Requirements:**
    ```
    curl -sL https://run.linkerd.io/install | sh
    export PATH=$PATH:${HOME}/.linkerd2/bin
    ```

    The above commands illustrate downloading and setting up the Linkerd CLI, a prerequisite toolkit that facilitates interaction with the mesh.

- **Network Configuration:** DNS resolution must be correctly configured within the cluster to permit internal service communication. Adequate egress and ingress rules ensure external communication is securely managed.

- **TLS and CertManager Certificates:** Supporting mTLS implicitly requires preparing CertManager, or similar mechanisms, for managing TLS certificates within the cluster. This factor is paramount when enterprises seek industry-standard service security.

**Network Infrastructure Needs:**

The network infrastructure further imposes requirements due to its influence on Linkerd's functionality. Minimization of latency and packet loss within the system benefits Linkerd's metrics and tracing capabilities.

- **Latency Requirements:** Low latency within the cluster is crucial as increased communication delay directly impacts the performance of service tracing and logging mechanisms such as distributed tracing services.

- **Bandwidth Considerations:** Although the bandwidth requirements are not substantial compared to large-scale application data flows, adequate bandwidth must be available to ensure seamless metric logging, especially during peak operational hours.

**Performance Implications and Sizing Guidelines**

Predicting Linkerd's impact on cluster resources in large deployments requires thorough performance testing.

**Load Testing:** Conducting load tests simulates high-traffic scenarios, enabling calibration of CPU and memory allocation within both control and data planes. The focus should remain on:

- Evaluating how Linkerd proxy performance changes with varying numbers of services and traffic volumes.

- Ensuring that metrics reporting remains accurate and efficient even as services scale.

**Scalability and Redundancy:** Depending on the deployment environment, adding redundancy to the control plane by deploying multiple replicas of Linkerd components may be necessary. This approach mitigates service disruptions during failures.

```
kubectl scale deploy/linkerd-controller --replicas=3
kubectl scale deploy/linkerd-web --replicas=2
```

Scaling deployments using Kubernetes 'kubectl' CLI commands ensures cluster resources meet dynamic application demands without degrading service mesh performance.

In tailoring these configurations, it is beneficial to anticipate growth by configuring resource limits and requests in Kubernetes manifests. Resource constraints ensure no single application monopolizes cluster resources.

Overall, understanding and addressing the system requirements for Linkerd are fundamental for its integration into any Kubernetes environment. These requirements guide resource allocation, inform network configuration changes, and prepare for scalability, which collectively empowers system architects and developers in deploying highly efficient, resilient applications within service mesh ecosystems.

## 3.2 Installing Linkerd CLI

The Linkerd Command Line Interface (CLI) acts as a crucial tool for developers and operators working with the Linkerd service mesh. It provides an intuitive interface for performing vital actions such as installation, upgrades, diagnostics, and interaction with the Linkerd control plane. By facilitating these tasks efficiently, the CLI becomes an indispensable component of the service mesh ecosystem. This section offers an extensive exploration of the Linkerd CLI installation process, covering the steps required across various operating systems, accompanied by insights into its utilization and configuration.

## Environment Preparations

Before initiating the installation of the Linkerd CLI, there are essential preparatory steps necessary to ensure a smooth process. These include verifying system compatibility and ensuring internet access for downloading necessary components.

**System Compatibility:**

The CLI's compatibility with diverse operating systems like Linux, macOS, and Windows streamlines cross-platform management. Each platform requires specific installation steps outlined as follows:

- **Linux Systems:** Most Linux distributions support the CLI, including popular ones such as Ubuntu, Debian, and CentOS.

- **macOS:** The CLI is compatible with recent versions of macOS, utilizing package managers like Homebrew for straightforward installation.

- **Windows:** Windows setups often employ tools like Cygwin or Windows Subsystem for Linux (WSL) for native-like CLI functionality.

**Prerequisite Tools:**

Prior to installing the Linkerd CLI, ensure that critical command-line utilities such as 'curl' or 'wget' and 'tar' are available, since they facilitate the fetching and unpacking of CLI archives from the internet. Tools can be verified and installed using system package managers:

```
# For Debian-based systems
sudo apt update
sudo apt install curl wget tar

# For CentOS systems
sudo yum install curl wget tar
```

## Installing Linkerd CLI on Linux

For Linux-based systems, the Linkerd CLI installation process is straightforward. Below, we provide step-by-step details utilizing the 'curl' command followed by archive unpacking:

```
# Fetch the linkerd install script
curl -sL https://run.linkerd.io/install | sh
```

## 3.2. INSTALLING LINKERD CLI

The command fetches and executes a script that downloads the Linkerd binary to your path, adapting depending on user preferences. Subsequently, add the CLI binary directory to the system's 'PATH':

```
# Add linkerd binary to PATH
export PATH=$PATH:$HOME/.linkerd2/bin
```

The 'PATH' modification ensures that the 'linkerd' command is globally accessible across sessions. To ensure a persistent path beyond terminal sessions, add the line to '.bashrc' or ' /.profile':

```
# Persist PATH in .bashrc
echo 'export PATH=$PATH:$HOME/.linkerd2/bin' >> ~/.bashrc
source ~/.bashrc
```

## Installing Linkerd CLI on macOS Using Homebrew

On macOS, Homebrew provides a simple method for installing the Linkerd CLI. This package manager simplifies application management on UNIX-based systems:

```
# Ensure Homebrew is up-to-date
brew update

# Install Linkerd CLI using Homebrew
brew install linkerd

# Verification
linkerd version
```

Running 'linkerd version' post-installation will verify the CLI's presence and show its current version, confirming successful setup.

## Installing Linkerd CLI on Windows

For Windows, using the Windows Subsystem for Linux (WSL) can facilitate a native Linux-like environment, easing the installation of the Linkerd CLI. Assuming WSL is already enabled, with a distribution installed:

```
# Open WSL terminal
# Import and run Linkerd install script in WSL
curl -sL https://run.linkerd.io/install | sh
```

```
# Add linkerd to PATH in WSL environment
echo 'export PATH=$PATH:$HOME/.linkerd2/bin' >> ~/.bashrc
source ~/.bashrc
```

Alternatively, developers can use 'scoop', another package manager, to install Linkerd CLI directly on Windows. 'scoop' provides a comfortable approach without incorporating a full Linux subsystem:

```
# Ensure scoop is installed
scoop update

# Install Linkerd CLI with scoop
scoop install linkerd

# Verification
linkerd version
```

## Verifying the Linkerd CLI Installation

Regardless of the operating system, verifying the installation of the Linkerd CLI is vital. Users can employ the 'linkerd check' command, which evaluates whether all necessary settings for an ideal setup are in place:

```
# Run linkerd check to validate setup
linkerd check --pre
```

This command guides users by highlighting potential aspects necessitating remediation before further actions like deploying the service mesh within a Kubernetes cluster.

The 'linkerd check' diagnostic tool forms part of a broader suite for preflight checking, boasting automated insight generation that solves deviations promptly.

## Using the Linkerd CLI for Basic Commands

Once installed, the Linkerd CLI affords users the ability to manage and troubleshoot Linkerd installations. Essential commands available include:

- **Installing Linkerd on a Kubernetes Cluster:**

```
# Install Linkerd onto Kubernetes
```

```
linkerd install | kubectl apply -f -

# Validate successful deployment
linkerd check
```

- **Upgrade Procedure:**

Upgrading Linkerd deployments hinges on initiating the command 'linkerd upgrade' to ensure current installations receive the latest compatible updates adhering to cluster policies and best practices.

- **Traffic Splitting and Management:**

Through the CLI, users execute advanced features such as traffic-split, effectively distributing traffic between multiple service versions for canary deployments and performance monitoring.

The installation and operational fluency with the Linkerd CLI dramatically streamline service mesh management, effectively reducing complexities intertwined with microservice applications. Chain processes (like initial installations, upgrades, and management) reveal CLI capability as a pivotal constituent in the Linkerd lifecycle, reinforcing observability, security, and resilience across all service endpoints.

## 3.3 Setting Up Linkerd on Kubernetes

Setting up Linkerd on a Kubernetes cluster involves deploying the service mesh control plane components and configuring the data plane proxies for optimal interaction with microservices. This process not only orchestrates the integration of Linkerd into the Kubernetes environment but also provides additional layers of observability, reliability, and security. This section presents comprehensive guidelines for deploying Linkerd onto a Kubernetes cluster, offering insights into deployment strategies, configuration adjustments, and best practices to enhance performance and usability.

Prior to deploying Linkerd on Kubernetes, it is necessary to ensure that several prerequisites are fulfilled:

**1. Kubernetes Cluster:**

A functional Kubernetes cluster is a foundational requirement. Depending on deployment targets, the cluster could reside on-premises, in a cloud environment such as AWS, GCP, or Azure, or in a hybrid setup.

- **Kubernetes Version:** Ensure the Kubernetes version meets Linkerd's compatibility requirements, typically the last few versions supported. For instance, Linkerd v2.x requires Kubernetes 1.19 or newer.

- **Access Credentials:** Using kubectl, the Kubernetes command-line tool, administrators should confirm they have the necessary credentials and permissions to deploy workloads within the cluster.

```
# Verify Kubernetes context and access
kubectl config current-context
kubectl cluster-info
```

### 2. Linkerd CLI:

As an essential tool, the Linkerd CLI should be installed and configured correctly. This tool enables users to execute Linkerd-specific commands including installation, check, and metrics collection.

### 3. Sufficient Resource Allocation:

Verify that node capacity within the cluster can efficiently support Linkerd's resource requirements, taking into account the additional load from the service mesh.

### Deploying the Linkerd Control Plane

Deploying the Linkerd control plane involves utilizing the Linkerd CLI to inject the required control plane components into the Kubernetes cluster. These components will manage service mesh operations including metrics collection, policy enforcement, and mTLS.

### 1. Install Linkerd Control Plane:

The deployment begins with executing the linkerd install command, which configures the necessary Kubernetes manifests. These manifests elucidate the control plane's desired state within the Kubernetes API.

```
# Install Linkerd Control Plane
linkerd install | kubectl apply -f -
```

The above command targets the default Kubernetes namespace unless otherwise specified through additional arguments or namespace flags.

## 3.3. SETTING UP LINKERD ON KUBERNETES

\*\*Control Plane Components:\*\*

- **Controller:** Responsible for managing service proxies and coordinating updates. - **Prometheus:** Collects metrics from the proxies and provides vital observability data. - **Grafana:** Enables visualization of collected metrics through comprehensive dashboards. - **Web:** A user-facing dashboard providing a high-level view of service mesh health.

### 2. Validate Installation:

Following the initial deployment, administrators should confirm the successful installation of the control plane by executing critical diagnostic commands from the CLI:

```
# Validate Control Plane Setup
linkerd check
```

Verification through linkerd check performs an assortment of validity tests across deployed components, confirming their operational status and readiness for integration with service workloads.

### Configuring the Linkerd Data Plane

The Linkerd data plane consists of lightweight proxies co-located with each Kubernetes service pod. These proxies handle traffic routing, observability, and security enforcement between services.

### 1. Inject Proxies into Services:

Linkerd leverages a process called "proxy injection," where it injects a sidecar container (the proxy) into Kubernetes pods. The sidecar intercepts inbound and outbound network traffic on behalf of the primary service container.

```
# Apply Linkerd Proxy Injection to Deployment
linkerd inject deployment.yaml | kubectl apply -f -
```

This action alters specified deployments by including the proxy container in the pod template, updating them inline or through a separate file.

\*\*Automatic Proxy Injection:\*\*

Linkerd supports enabling automatic proxy injection. This mechanism requires annotating the desired namespaces or configurations within the cluster:

CHAPTER 3. INSTALLING AND CONFIGURING LINKERD

```
# Enable automatic injection for a namespace
kubectl annotate namespace default linkerd.io/inject=enabled
```

## 2. Configure Traffic Policies:

As part of Linkerd's security model, configuring network policies allows developers to define service communication rules. The use of mTLS (mutual TLS) ensures that all service-to-service communication remains encrypted and authenticated:

- **mTLS Configuration:** By default, Linkerd activates mTLS, requiring no additional configuration. However, detailed setups may involve establishing trust roots or managing custom certificate rotations through cert-manager integrations.

- **Traffic Splitting:** Linkerd affords users the ability to split traffic between service versions. This functionality is vital for canary releases, facilitating gradual rollouts and monitoring based on real user interactions.

```
# Define a TrafficSplit for balancing between versions
apiVersion: split.smi-spec.io/v1alpha2
kind: TrafficSplit
metadata:
  name: my-service-split
spec:
  service: my-service
  backends:
  - service: my-service-v1
    weight: 500m
  - service: my-service-v2
    weight: 500m
```

## Advanced Configuration and Scalability

Upon the initial setup, it is essential to tune Linkerd configurations to maximize resource usage efficiency and operational scalability:

### 1. Resource Management:

Administrators should leverage Kubernetes' resource requests and limits to define how resources are allocated and constrained to prevent resource starvation:

```
# Example pod manifest with resource constraints
apiVersion: v1
kind: Pod
metadata:
  name: my-pod
```

## 3.3. SETTING UP LINKERD ON KUBERNETES

```
spec:
  containers:
  - name: my-container
    image: my-image
    resources:
      requests:
        cpu: "250m"
        memory: "64Mi"
      limits:
        cpu: "500m"
        memory: "128Mi"
```

**Monitoring and Observability:**

The robust metric collection facilitated by Linkerd allows teams to observe service health and performance. By integrating dashboards and alerts through Prometheus and Grafana, operators gain actionable visibility into metrics.

**2. Horizontal Scaling:**

Scaling workloads horizontally can aid in accommodating increased traffic while maintaining service quality. Kubernetes provides the Horizontal Pod Autoscaler (HPA) which uses metrics collected by Linkerd's Prometheus for real-time scaling decisions:

```
# Configuring HPA based on CPU utilization
apiVersion: autoscaling/v2beta2
kind: HorizontalPodAutoscaler
metadata:
  name: my-deployment-hpa
spec:
  scaleTargetRef:
    apiVersion: apps/v1
    kind: Deployment
    name: my-deployment
  minReplicas: 2
  maxReplicas: 5
  metrics:
  - type: Resource
    resource:
      name: cpu
      target:
        type: Utilization
        averageUtilization: 50
```

Comprehensive understanding of these configurations ensures Linkerd operates seamlessly, exhibiting robust performance and scalability in real-world scenarios. Such setups transform service mesh architecture, leveraging Kubernetes' strengths in orchestrating secure, observable, and reliable microservices clusters. Deploying Linkerd within Kubernetes not only refines service deployment strategies but galvanizes operational agility for developers and engineers navigating the modern application landscape.

## 3.4 Verifying the Installation

Verifying the installation of Linkerd within a Kubernetes cluster is a fundamental process that ensures all service mesh components are correctly deployed and functional. This verification step is crucial to preemptively detecting and addressing any misconfigurations or irregularities that could impede system performance or reliability. This section delves into the methods and best practices for validating the successful installation of Linkerd, encompassing inspection strategies, diagnostic commands, and enhanced troubleshooting techniques with an emphasis on ensuring robust service mesh operations.

The Linkerd CLI is the cornerstone of the verification process, offering comprehensive command-line tools to audit the installation against expected configurations and health metrics. The primary command used for verification is `linkerd check`.

```
# Running linkerd check to verify installation
linkerd check
```

Executing `linkerd check` performs a sequence of health checks on the Linkerd control plane and data plane components. The results are systematically tabulated, detailing which components have met expectations and flagging anomalies that warrant remedial actions.

The health of deployed components can be systematically analyzed through metrics and logs accessible via Kubernetes and Linkerd-provided interfaces. Key components examined include:

**1. Linkerd Control Plane:**

The control plane manages mesh operations and necessitates consistent monitoring to ensure its components such as controller, identity, and web remain healthy and performant.

- **Prometheus Metrics:** Integrated Prometheus provides access to control plane metrics. Using `kubectl port-forward`, the

## 3.4. VERIFYING THE INSTALLATION

Prometheus service becomes accessible for querying metrics:

```
# Forward Prometheus service port to localhost
kubectl -n linkerd port-forward svc/linkerd-prometheus 9090:9090
```

- **Grafana:** With metrics forwarded, Grafana visualizations offer a vivid perspective on control plane health. Accessing dashboards through port-forwarding:

```
# Access Grafana dashboard
kubectl -n linkerd port-forward svc/linkerd-grafana 3000:3000
```

**2. Linkerd Data Plane Proxies:**

The health of proxies deployed with application workloads is imperative to ensure consistent traffic management, security, and observability. Inspect individual namespace health through:

```
# Checking data plane proxy status in a namespace
linkerd -n [namespace] check --proxy
```

This command scrutinizes each proxy for alignment with desired operational states, displaying findings in a structured format conducive to rapid diagnostics.

Log files provide real-time insights into operational states and diagnostics of running components. Two principal logging strategies involve leveraging Kubernetes log management capabilities:

**1. Accessing Linkerd Logs:**

Access logs directly from Linkerd deployments to explore runtime events and troubleshooting information. This is essential to understanding real-time Proxy or Control Plane component behaviors:

```
# Display logs for Linkerd controller
kubectl -n linkerd logs deploy/linkerd-controller
```

Such logs uncover anomalies such as restart loops, certificate misconfigurations, or network connectivity issues.

**2. Using Log Aggregation Tooling:**

Modern Kubernetes clusters benefit from centralized log aggregation through tools like Fluentd, Elk Stack, or Amazon CloudWatch. These solutions provide consolidated views of log data across entire environments, improving user capabilities in correlational analyses and historical log examination.

Linkerd's architecture readily integrates with advanced monitoring and diagnostic tools, bolstering its observability and troubleshooting prowess:

**1. Distributed Tracing:**

Understanding service-to-service communication latency and flow requires careful analysis through distributed tracing tools. Linkerd supports integration with OpenTracing-compatible systems, such as Jaeger:

- **Jaeger Integration:** Easily visualize traces across the service mesh to recalibrate performance and fault-tolerance strategies, especially during high-load conditions.

    ```
    # Port-forward Jaeger UI
    kubectl port-forward svc/jaeger-query 16686:16686
    ```

    Visualize service dependencies and latency, enabling teams to identify bottlenecks or sub-optimal communication patterns promptly.

**2. Using Kiali for Service Mesh Visualization:**

Kiali provides an interactive view of the service mesh, depicting topology, traffic distribution, and error states. Deploy Kiali within the same cluster to complement Grafana metrics with intuitive service interaction models:

```
# Install Kiali for visual service mesh monitoring
kubectl apply -f https://raw.githubusercontent.com/kiali/kiali-operator/master/deploy/kubernetes/kiali.yaml
```

Kiali assists in delineating service connectivity, verifying endpoint health, and reinforcing the understanding of metrics' interconnections.

Despite thorough preparatory steps, installations can encounter various concerns that complicate Linkerd's effective establishment.

**1. Addressing Networking Issues:**

Network configurations underpinning service navigation across the

## 3.4. VERIFYING THE INSTALLATION

mesh must be routinely verified. Commonly encountered issues include DNS misconfigurations or incompatible CNI plugins impacting service discovery and routing:

- **CNI Plugin Compatibility:** Confirm compatibility of network plugins with Linkerd as certain legacy or patched plugins may disrupt proxy communication. Consider switching to CNI solutions aligned with Linkerd's recommended specifications.

- **Service Discovery:** Utilize the service discovery capabilities of Kubernetes CoreDNS. Adjust CoreDNS configurations to rectify errors when services fail to resolve names correctly.

**2. Resolving Control Plane Configurations:**

Control Plane anomalies often stem from environmental misconfigurations:

- **Certificates and Identity:** Address mTLS issues by ensuring that root certificates are correctly configured, conforming to validation policies stipulated in Linkerd's identity management.

- **Cluster Role Bindings:** Confirm role-based access controls (RBAC) are consistently applied, ensuring both control and data plane entities possess necessary privileges to operate efficiently.

A comprehensive understanding and execution of these verification techniques not only confirms the complete and correct installation of Linkerd but fosters a stable environment conducive to reliable service mesh functionality. Implementing smart verification and rapid remediation enables development teams and operators to trust in the robustness of their service mesh architectures, paving a seamless path towards their enterprise application's agile deployment and management.

## 3.5 Configuring Linkerd for Your Environment

Effective configuration of Linkerd for specific environments is paramount to taking advantage of its full suite of features, aligning with organizational requirements, and optimizing performance. Configuring Linkerd involves tailoring it to the operational characteristics of the underlying infrastructure, ensuring compliance with security protocols, and enhancing observability. This section provides a comprehensive guide to configuring Linkerd, with insights into adapting it for diverse deployment scenarios and organization-specific needs.

Environmental adaptation and resource customization are essential for Linkerd's performance, which is intimately tied to the characteristics of its environment. Adapting configurations to fit the unique attributes of cloud-native, on-premises, or hybrid deployments is the first step in optimizing its functionality.

**1. Tailoring Resource Requests and Limits:**

Embarking on resource customization entails configuring Kubernetes' native resource requests and limits, which define the computational resources allocated to Linkerd components.

- **Control Plane:**

    Adjust resource allocations for Control Plane components, which include the Linkerd controller, proxy injector, web, and identity components. This ensures availability without risking resource wastage:

    ```
    # Example configuration for Control Plane resource allocation
    apiVersion: apps/v1
    kind: Deployment
    metadata:
      name: linkerd-controller
    spec:
      template:
        spec:
          containers:
          - name: controller
            resources:
              requests:
                cpu: "100m"
    ```

### 3.5. CONFIGURING LINKERD FOR YOUR ENVIRONMENT

```
      memory: "256Mi"
   limits:
      cpu: "500m"
      memory: "512Mi"
```

- **Data Plane:**

  Similarly, requests and limits for the data plane proxies must reflect anticipated traffic loads, with adjustments made for spikes during peak demand periods.

**2. Scaling Considerations:**

Scaling strategies hinge on dynamic adaptations of component replicas to accommodate increased load or traffic. Horizontal Pod Autoscaling is leveraged to dynamically scale Linkerd proxies in response to service activity:

```
# Horizontal scaling configuration using HPA
apiVersion: autoscaling/v2
kind: HorizontalPodAutoscaler
metadata:
  name: proxy-autoscaler
spec:
  scaleTargetRef:
    apiVersion: apps/v1
    kind: Deployment
    name: linkerd-proxy
  minReplicas: 2
  maxReplicas: 10
  metrics:
  - type: Resource
    resource:
      name: cpu
      target:
        type: Utilization
        averageUtilization: 75
```

Networking and security considerations are pivotal when configuring Linkerd, as they directly influence communication flows and service integrity.

**1. Mutual TLS (mTLS) Configuration:**

Securing inter-service communication using mTLS is a quintessential feature for Linkerd. Carefully configured, mTLS encrypts data in transit, guaranteeing authenticity verification for all service interactions:

- **Certificate Management:**

Configuring certificates involves setting trust chain validity and rotation policies. This can be achieved by integrating with 'cert-manager' for automated certificate issuance and renewal to simplify lifecycle management:

```
# Enable cert-manager integration
kubectl apply -f https://github.com/jetstack/cert-manager/releases/
    download/v1.5.3/cert-manager.crds.yaml

# Define certificate issuer and resources
kubectl apply -f issuer-config.yaml
```

- **Fine-Grained Network Policy Creation:**

  Network policies enforce granular traffic flow control across the Kubernetes network, preventing unauthorized service interactions and policing data exchange:

```
# Define a network policy to restrict ingress to a namespace
apiVersion: networking.k8s.io/v1
kind: NetworkPolicy
metadata:
  name: allow-ingress-from-namespace
spec:
  podSelector:
    matchLabels:
      app: myapp
  ingress:
  - from:
    - namespaceSelector:
        matchLabels:
          name: trusted-namespace
```

Such policies define which namespaces or pods can initiate communication, vital in compliance-bound industries to ensure adherence to security mandates.

## 2. Observability Enhancement:

Prometheus and Grafana integrate seamlessly with Linkerd, extending observability into performance metrics, logs, and traces.

- **Enhanced Metrics Collection:**

  Leveraging custom metrics and alerting capabilities informs on deviations from normatively defined operational thresholds, boosting situational awareness:

## 3.5. CONFIGURING LINKERD FOR YOUR ENVIRONMENT

```
# Sample PrometheusRules configuration for Linkerd alerts
apiVersion: monitoring.coreos.com/v1
kind: PrometheusRule
metadata:
  name: linkerd-alerts
spec:
  groups:
  - name: linkerd-metrics.rules
    rules:
    - alert: HighLatency
      expr: sum(linkerd_http_request_duration_seconds_bucket{
          namespace="default"}) by (status) > 5
      for: 5m
      labels:
        severity: warning
      annotations:
        summary: "High request latency detected"
        description: "The latency of requests is exceeding expected
            thresholds."
```

- **Distributed Tracing:**

    Configuring tracing agents such as Jaeger or OpenTelemetry enables correlation of microservice interactions, yielding insights into bottleneck identification and system behavior optimization.

Opportunities abound for customizing Linkerd installations to align with organizational frameworks, spanning compliance, operational efficiency, and strategic goals.

### 1. Integration with CI/CD Pipelines:

End-to-end deployment strategies involve integrating mesh configurations with CI/CD tools, enabling seamless automated deployments and rollbacks:

- Use GitOps principles where repository changes trigger configuration updates.

- Employ Helm charts to represent Linkerd infrastructure as code, permitting straightforward alterations and re-deployments as needed:

```
# Initializing a Linkerd Helm chart deployment
helm repo add linkerd https://helm.linkerd.io/stable
helm install linkerd-control-plane linkerd/linkerd2
```

Industries subject to stringent data protection regulations necessitate specific configurative efforts to ensure full auditability beside R&D conformity:

- Maintain logs and observability records compliant with data protection policies.
- Regularly audit component configurations, applying organization-specific policy controls utilizing Raft or Istio's Galley to ensure adherence to pre-defined standards.

Multi-cluster strategies often yield scalability and resilience, especially for globally distributed environments or disaster recovery purposes.

When configuring Linkerd for multi-cluster operationality, factor in the following:

**1. Cluster Gateways and Cross-Cluster Traffic Management:**

Configure gateways to facilitate traffic flows between independent service clusters, ensuring communication fidelity while allowing distinctive per-cluster customizations:

```
# Example cluster gateway configuration
apiVersion: linkerd.io/v1alpha1
kind: ServiceProfile
metadata:
  name: my-service.default.svc.cluster.local
spec:
  gateway:
    selectors:
    - matchLabels:
        gateway: cross-cluster-gateway
```

**2. Unified Observability Across Clusters:**

Centralize log aggregation and metrics collection from the disparate clusters to ensure consistent observability using tools like Thanos for Prometheus metric aggregation.

By intricately configuring Linkerd to the nuances of your Kubernetes environments, teams can unlock unprecedented levels of service mesh functionality. These bespoke configurations not only guarantee that Linkerd aligns with organization-specific expectations but also enhance service reliability, resilience, and security across microservice architectures. The readiness to adapt Linkerd to evolving technological landscapes remains assured, laying a structured foundation for future operational excellence and scalability.

## 3.6 Updating and Maintaining Linkerd

The effective management of Linkerd within a Kubernetes ecosystem necessitates a keen focus on both the updating and maintenance of the service mesh. Ensuring modernized deployments that are attuned to the latest feature sets and security optimizations requires a proactive approach towards updates. Concurrently, steadfast maintenance routines guarantee operational integrity, resilience, and peak performance. This section outlines the detailed processes of updating Linkerd, considerations for compatibility and compliance, as well as strategies for maintaining a reliable service mesh architecture.

The Importance of Regular Updates

Regular updates are critical for ensuring that Linkerd deployments benefit from ongoing advancements in security protocols, performance enhancements, and feature expansions. Updates often address vulnerabilities that could otherwise compromise service interactions or system stability. They introduce innovations that enhance observability, reliability, and ease of use across evolving Kubernetes environments.

Version Compatibility and Pre-Update Preparations

Updating Linkerd begins with an assessment of version compatibility, ensuring that any changes do not inadvertently disrupt service continuity.

**1. Reviewing the Update's Impact:**

Each new release of Linkerd is accompanied by detailed release notes that catalog significant changes, deprecated functionalities, and migration paths. It is imperative to thoroughly review these notes to understand the impact on existing configurations and service dependencies.

**2. Pre-Update Checklist:**

Prior to initiating updates, perform the following:

- Backup Configurations: Ensure that current configurations, including custom resource definitions (CRDs) and Kubernetes YAML files, are backed up to prevent data loss during the update process.

- Test Updates in a Staging Environment: Deploy the update in a non-production environment to identify potential issues.

- Check Downtime Metrics: Evaluate anticipated downtime and establish mitigation steps to lessen user impact.

```
# Export configuration beforehand
kubectl get crd > crd-backup.yaml
kubectl get ns -o yaml > ns-backup.yaml
```

Executing the Update Process

Linkerd updates can be accomplished utilizing the Linkerd CLI and Helm, each method offering distinct advantages based on deployment complexity and preference.

**1. CLI-Based Update:**

Using the CLI is a direct approach for smaller or less-complex environments. Ensure the CLI version aligns with the intended Linkerd version update.

- Upgrade Command Execution:

```
# Linkerd Upgrade
linkerd upgrade | kubectl apply -f -
linkerd check
```

The command replaces existing control plane resources with updated specifications, preserving custom configurations where applicable.

- Version Verification:

Post-update verification ensures the control plane functions correctly. The 'linkerd check' command confirms state consensus across updated components, verifying successful rollout without regressions.

**2. Helm-Based Update:**

## 3.6. UPDATING AND MAINTAINING LINKERD

For environments originally deployed using Helm, employing Helm charts for updates affords concise control over version management and rollback procedures.

- Update with Helm:

```
# Update Helm repo
helm repo update

# Upgrade Linkerd using Helm
helm upgrade --install linkerd-control-plane linkerd/linkerd2 -f values.yaml
```

Configuring values in 'values.yaml' according to environment-specific requirements ensures continuity of custom configurations through updates.

Maintaining Linkerd for Performance and Reliability

Once updated, maintaining Linkerd involves routine actions to ensure optimal operation and proactive resolution of issues.

1. **Monitoring and Performance Tuning:**

Continual access to observability metrics via Prometheus and Grafana is invaluable for identifying performance bottlenecks and planning capacity expansions when necessary.

- Identify Key Metrics:

Utilize Linkerd's comprehensive suite of metrics to monitor aspects such as request latencies, success rates, and proxy traffic volumes.

```
# Sample script to query Prometheus for request latency
curl -G http://localhost:9090/api/v1/query --data-urlencode 'query=sum(rate(
    linkerd_request_duration_bucket[5m])) by (status)'
```

- Automate Alerts:

Configure alerts for critical metrics surpassing predetermined thresholds, prompting immediate administrative action:

```
# Alert rule configuration
groups:
  - name: linkerd-alerts
```

```
rules:
- alert: HighErrorRate
  expr: sum(rate(linkerd_http_request_errors_total[5m])) by (namespace) > 0.1
  for: 10m
  labels:
    severity: critical
  annotations:
    summary: "High error rate detected"
```

## 2. Scalability Enhancements:

Linkerd's scalability facilitates adapting to increased traffic loads through horizontal and vertical scaling practices, with Kubernetes' autoscaling tools providing dynamic resource allocation:

```
# Horizontal Pod Autoscaling example with metrics integration
apiVersion: autoscaling/v2beta2
kind: HorizontalPodAutoscaler
metadata:
  name: linkerd-controller-hpa
spec:
  scaleTargetRef:
    apiVersion: apps/v1
    kind: Deployment
    name: linkerd-controller
  minReplicas: 2
  maxReplicas: 10
  metrics:
  - type: Resource
    resource:
      name: cpu
      target:
        type: Utilization
        averageUtilization: 70
```

## 3. Security Practices:

Security vigilance within Linkerd involves continuously auditing access policies, mTLS configurations, and RBAC roles.

- Periodic Certificate Rotations:

Automated systems for routine mTLS certificates rotation ensure uninterrupted, valid cryptographic exchanges across the mesh:

```
# Certificate rotation with cert-manager
kubectl exec cert-manager -- cert-manager certificate renew
```

- RBAC Review:

## 3.6. UPDATING AND MAINTAINING LINKERD

Evaluate and update Role-Based Access Control policies to circumvent superfluous access privileges and apply least-privilege principles accurately.

Troubleshooting and Documentation Practices

Adopting rigorous documentation and troubleshooting methodologies improve maintenance efficacy:

**1. Documentation Updates:**

Maintain clear, detailed documentation reflecting version changes and environment-specific adjustments. Highlight novel configurations, altered workflows, and results of testing updates.

**2. Diagnostic Protocols:**

Establish comprehensive diagnostic protocols identifying failures originating from updates. Capture logs and metric samples immediately before and after upgrading for granular impact assessments:

```
# Capturing logs for review
kubectl logs deploy/linkerd-controller > controller-pre-update.log
kubectl logs deploy/linkerd-controller > controller-post-update.log
```

The ongoing management and updating of Linkerd are pivotal to sustaining an agile, high-performance service mesh in dynamic Kubernetes environments. Regular updates, fortified by robust maintenance practices and systematic performance evaluation, equip service infrastructures to harness evolving technological advancements efficiently and securely. By meticulously following outlined procedures, any organization can leverage Linkerd's full potential, reinforcing reliable and innovative microservice ecosystems.

# Chapter 4

# Core Features of Linkerd

Linkerd stands out for its array of core features designed to enhance the management of microservices communication. This chapter provides an in-depth look at Linkerd's capabilities, including traffic routing and load balancing, which are crucial for distributing workloads efficiently. It also explores observability features that facilitate metrics collection and real-time monitoring. Security is addressed through automatic mutual TLS encryption, ensuring secure communication between services. Failover mechanisms and latency management are highlighted, showcasing how Linkerd improves resilience and performance. Together, these features empower users to build robust, reliable, and secure service mesh infrastructures.

## 4.1 Traffic Routing and Load Balancing

In microservices architectures, efficient traffic routing and load balancing are pivotal for ensuring optimal service performance and availability. Linkerd, as a service mesh, is designed to handle the complexities associated with traffic management across distributed services. This section delves into the methodologies employed by Linkerd to route traffic and balance loads effectively, ensuring a smooth operation within a microservices environment.

Linkerd operates as an application layer proxy designed to route and balance traffic across service endpoints. It introduces a decentralized model for managing how requests are distributed across various services, leveraging sophisticated algorithms to minimize latency and maximize throughput.

The architecture of Linkerd includes a data plane and a control plane. The data plane, which is injected as a sidecar proxy alongside every service instance, is responsible for managing the actual traffic between services. Conversely, the control plane provides configuration and management of the service mesh. These components work in tandem to facilitate intelligent and adaptive routing strategies.

**Traffic Routing:**

Linkerd's routing entails directing incoming requests to the appropriate service instances. The routing mechanism is built on top of the Service Profile of each service, which defines expected behaviors and performance characteristics. Service Profiles inform Linkerd about the endpoints that exist for a particular service and any specific routes such as path-based routing or method-based routing, it must be aware of.

Linkerd primarily uses the URL's path or method specified in Service Profiles to match the incoming requests to the service's specific endpoint. The importance of this method of routing lies in its ability to route based on HTTP methods, body, and headers, thereby enabling finer control and granularity of traffic management.

For efficient URL-based routing, the following Linkerd Service Profile could be defined to route the request to desired endpoints:

```
apiVersion: linkerd.io/v1alpha2
kind: ServiceProfile
metadata:
  name: service-namespace.service.svc.cluster.local
spec:
  routes:
  - name: GET /
    condition:
      method: GET
      pathRegex: /home
```

```
- name: POST /signup
  condition:
    method: POST
    pathRegex: /user/signup
```

The example above exhibits how HTTP requests to paths '/home' and '/user/signup' are routed based on HTTP methods GET and POST respectively.

**Load Balancing:**

Load balancing, the equitable distribution of traffic load across service instances, is paramount in microservices architectures. Linkerd incorporates advanced load balancing methods to distribute incoming requests seamlessly, preventing any single service instance from becoming a bottleneck or potential point of failure.

Linkerd employs a sophisticated load balancing strategy called *least-request*, which dynamically balances incoming requests based on real-time performance metrics, such as response latency and success rates of service instances. This algorithm inspects the in-flight requests across instances and routes a new request to the instance handling the fewest requests at any given point. This approach helps maintain optimal resource utilization and minimizes request queuing and waiting times.

Additionally, Linkerd's load balancing can be fine-tuned through configuration settings in the service mesh, which allows for adjustments based on specific use cases and performance needs of the services.

```
config:
  loadBalancer:
    strategy: least-request
    maxRequests: 100
    ewmaUpdatePeriodMs: 10
```

The *least-request* strategy is configurable with parameters such as maxRequests which defines the threshold of outstanding requests an instance may handle before the balancer favors another instance, and ewmaUpdatePeriodMs which establishes how frequently the estimated weighted moving average is updated for balancing.

**Fault Tolerance and Resilience:**

Linkerd's integration of traffic routing and load balancing directly contributes to the fault tolerance and resilience of microservices. By administering intelligent request management and routing around potential service instance failures or performance degradations, Linkerd ensures high availability and robustness of the system.

Consider scenarios where a service instance experiences elevated response times or begins returning higher error rates. Linkerd's load balancer can promptly redirect traffic to healthier instances, effectively isolating problematic instances and reducing user-perceived latency or errors.

**Better Traffic Management with Service Mesh:**

Service meshes like Linkerd provide the added advantage of enforcing consistency in traffic routing and load balancing across heterogeneous service environments. Regardless of the complexity or variations in service implementations, the service mesh uniformly manages inter-service communications, offering uniform visibility and control over traffic patterns.

This consistent traffic management enhances the operational simplicity for engineering teams, as they can define global traffic rules and policies enforced centrally by the service mesh. This centralized control helps in easily onboarding new services, scaling existing systems, or progressively deploying blue-green or canary releases with minimum risk of downtime.

**Canary and Blue-Green Deployments:**

Linkerd supports canary and blue-green deployment strategies, providing built-in capabilities for gradual service rollouts. This is achieved by defining traffic splitting policies within the Linkerd setup, thus enabling control over the percentage of live traffic directed to different versions of a service.

For instance, a new version of a service can be introduced, with a small percentage of requests initially routed to it. Monitoring and feedback can inform whether the new version is functioning correctly, allowing for traffic percentage scaling quickly or rollback in case issues arise.

```
apiVersion: split.smi-spec.io/v1alpha4
kind: TrafficSplit
metadata:
  name: canary-release
spec:
```

```
service: service-main
backends:
- service: service-v1
    weight: 80
- service: service-v2
    weight: 20
```

In this configuration, 80% of the traffic is directed to the stable version service-v1 and 20% is routed to a canary version service-v2, allowing a controlled rollout and detection of any unforeseen service problems.

The ability to manage traffic in such a nuanced manner empowers organizations to adopt agile practices while ensuring service stability and performance continuity.

In essence, Linkerd's capabilities in traffic routing and load balancing articulate a sophisticated solution for managing the distributed nature of microservices effectively. By ensuring enhanced performance and reliability, it enables developers and operators to focus more on evolving and scaling business functionalities rather than the intricacies of service interactions. The flexible and extensible nature of Linkerd makes it an invaluable asset for organizations aiming to streamline their transition to cloud-native architectures.

## 4.2 Observability and Metrics Collection

The complexity inherent in microservices architectures necessitates robust frameworks for observability and metrics collection. Discernibility into service performance, health, and interactions is crucial for maintaining operational efficiency and reliability. Linkerd, a prominent service mesh, equips users with comprehensive observability tools to effectively monitor, diagnose, and optimize service behavior within the mesh.

Observability in the context of a service mesh like Linkerd refers to the ability to understand the state of the system based on the outputs (metrics, logs, traces) it generates. For Linkerd, these outputs facilitate a detailed view into the mesh's behavior, performance, and issues, empowering developers and operators with actionable insights.

**Core Observability Features:**

Linkerd integrates several observability features directly into its architecture, providing a seamless experience for monitoring service performance and health:

- **Golden Metrics:** Linkerd automatically collects a set of essential metrics known as "golden metrics," which include success rate, request volume, and latency. These metrics serve as a baseline for understanding service performance and are pivotal in identifying anomalies.

- **Per-Route Metrics:** Detailed metrics can be collected at a more granular level thanks to Linkerd's per-route monitoring capabilities. By analyzing metrics on a particular route basis, users can better diagnose route-specific issues and optimize performance for individual service paths.

- **Automatic Tracing:** Linkerd offers automatic request tracing to track the path of each request as it traverses different services within the mesh. This capability assists in identifying bottlenecks and analyzing inter-service dependencies effectively.

- **Service Topology Visualization:** Linkerd provides visualizations of service dependencies and their interactions, aiding in understanding the topology of the microservices environment.

**Metrics Collection:**

Linkerd makes use of its robust proxy architecture to gather telemetry data for all inter-service communications happening within the service mesh. Telemetry data collection is non-intrusive, requiring no modifications to application code.

The data plane proxies in Linkerd collect metrics and forward these to the control plane, which aggregates and processes them. Key metrics include request success rates, latencies (P50, P95, P99), request volume, and more, with metrics categorized per service and per route. These metrics are available through Prometheus, an industry-standard monitoring and alerting toolkit.

To enable Prometheus scraping of Linkerd metrics, the following configuration snippet can be included in Prometheus configuration:

## 4.2. OBSERVABILITY AND METRICS COLLECTION

```
scrape_configs:
  - job_name: 'linkerd'
    static_configs:
      - targets: ['<linkerd-pod-ip>:<metrics-port>']
```

With this configuration, Prometheus can retrieve metrics from Linkerd, organizing them for visualization and alerting in platforms such as Grafana.

**Data Visualization:**

Once collected and aggregated, metrics are visualized to present a coherent depiction of service performance and reliability. Grafana dashboards can be constructed using Linkerd's metrics, offering insights into metrics trends over time, per-service metrics, route-specific metrics, and overall mesh health.

An example Grafana dashboard may include panels for visualizing request success rate, latency distribution, and error rate across services, aiding in identifying trends or deviations from expected behavior that may signify performance issues.

**Tracing for Deep Insights:**

Tracing, as facilitated by Linkerd, is a powerful mechanism for gaining deep visibility into service interactions and performance by recording the journey of requests traversing diverse services. Linkerd supports tracing integration with systems such as Jaeger or Zipkin, enabling detailed trace views.

Jaeger collects traces showing the full path of requests and the latencies at each service interaction point, thus allowing the detection of inter-service dependencies and performance bottlenecks. Implementing tracing in Linkerd involves enabling a configuration in the Linkerd Helm chart or CLI.

```
linkerd:
  tracing:
    enabled: true
    collectorSvcAddr: jaeger-agent.linkerd:6831
```

This configuration communicates with Jaeger, passing trace data that, when visualized, empowers detailed latency breakdowns and root cause analysis for performance issues.

## Log Aggregation and Analysis:

While Linkerd primarily focuses on metrics and tracing, integrating its observability stack with centralized log aggregation tools like ELK or Fluentd can further augment diagnostic capabilities. Logs from applications and the Linkerd control plane itself can provide indispensable context to metrics and traces, enhancing the clarity around service issues.

Log aggregation may also expose patterns or errors not easily identifiable through metrics or tracing alone, such as application-specific errors or exceptions not propagating through service-to-service communications.

## Real-Time Monitoring and Alerts:

Building alerting mechanisms based on Linkerd's metrics enables proactive management of service performance and reliability. Prometheus Alertmanager, in conjunction with Linkerd metrics, configures policies to actively monitor and alert on threshold-based events, such as high error rates, elevated latencies, or atypical traffic patterns.

```
groups:
- name: linkerd-rules
  rules:
  - alert: HighErrorRate
    expr: job:linkerd_controller:request_failure{namespace="linkerd"} > 0.05
    for: 5m
    labels:
      severity: critical
    annotations:
      summary: "High error rate detected"
      description: "The error rate in the Linkerd control plane exceeds 5\% over the
        past 5 minutes."
```

With appropriate alerting rules, operational teams are equipped to respond dynamically to service issues, mitigating potential disruptions before they manifest at a user level.

## Service Performance Optimization:

The aggregate effect of Linkerd's observability features is improved service performance through informed optimizations. By analyzing patterns and insights provided by collected metrics, service owners can identify potential performance enhancements and execute them efficiently. This process assists organizations in achieving a higher degree of operational excellence.

For example, metrics depicting consistent high latency for a service can lead to action items addressing inefficiencies within the code, updating service infrastructure, or refining request routing strategies.

**Scaling Observability:**

As environments grow, scalability of observability solutions becomes imperative. Linkerd, with its in-built support for scaling metrics collection and integrations, empowers users to maintain visibility as additional services and nodes are incorporated into the mesh. The service mesh abstracts these complexities, maintaining consistent visibility and control.

Through scalable observability, organizations can maintain operational oversight without resistance, catering to growing demands while ensuring service reliability.

Observability and metrics collection in Linkerd thus provide a comprehensive framework for understanding microservices environments, promoting visibility, reliability, and operational efficiency. By deepening insights into the behavior and interactions of services, Linkerd enables teams to build and sustain robust systems for their business needs, adapting to dynamic challenges with agility and confidence.

## 4.3 Automatic mTLS Encryption

Security is an essential aspect of any microservices architecture, particularly as services become increasingly distributed and complex. Ensuring secure communication between services is crucial to protecting sensitive data and maintaining the integrity of the application ecosystem. Automatic mutual TLS (mTLS) encryption, a key feature of Linkerd, provides a robust security mechanism for encrypting service-to-service communication within a service mesh.

mTLS is an enhancement over traditional SSL/TLS encryption. It ensures that both parties in a communication session — the client and the server — are authenticated, unlike standard TLS where only the server is authenticated. Through mTLS, Linkerd guarantees that encrypted communications occur exclusively between authenticated parties, mitigating risks associated with man-in-the-middle attacks and unauthorized access.

**Principles and Benefits of mTLS:**

- **Mutual Authentication:** mTLS enforces mutual authentication by requiring both client and server to possess and present valid certificates during the handshake process. This strengthens the verification process of both communication parties, ensuring that only legitimate services within the mesh can communicate with each other.

- **Data Integrity and Confidentiality:** TLS encryption ensures that data transmitted across the network remains confidential and unaltered. mTLS extends this capability by authenticating endpoints, establishing a secure channel that protects data from interception or tampering.

- **Zero Trust Security Model:** Linkerd's use of mTLS aligns with the zero trust security paradigm, which assumes that threats can exist both inside and outside the network. By requiring strict authentication and encryption for every communication within the mesh, Linkerd creates a more secure microservices environment.

- **Automated Key and Certificate Management:** One of the paramount challenges of implementing mTLS is managing certificates and encryption keys. Linkerd automates this process, simplifying operations by managing the lifecycle of keys and certificates, performing routine rotation, and minimizing the risk of human error.

**How Linkerd Implements mTLS:**

Linkerd implements mTLS at the proxy level within its data plane, intercepting and managing all incoming and outgoing service traffic transparently. This ensures that mTLS is applied consistently without requiring explicit configuration or modification in individual service codebases.

The workflow of establishing mTLS in Linkerd involves several key stages:

## 4.3. AUTOMATIC MTLS ENCRYPTION

- **Certificate Issuance:** Upon installation, Linkerd generates its own root certificate authority (CA). This CA issues short-lived, service-specific certificates that facilitate mutual authentication across all services.

- **TLS Handshake:** The Linkerd proxy initiates a TLS handshake when establishing a connection between services. During this handshake, both the client and server proxies present their respective certificates. The root CA verifies the authenticity of these certificates, ensuring mutual trust before proceeding with communication.

- **Encryption and Decryption:** Upon successful authentication, a symmetric key is agreed upon by both parties, establishing a secure channel for encrypted data transmission. This key is used for encrypting and decrypting data as long as the connection persists.

- **Certificate Rotation:** Linkerd ensures certificates are short-lived (lasting for typically a day), automating their rotation. This reduces the possibility of key compromise and ensures long-term security with minimal administrative overhead.

**Configuration of mTLS in Linkerd:**

The mTLS feature in Linkerd is enabled by default, requiring minimal configuration. During installation or upgrade of the Linkerd control plane, the CLI or Helm might be used to define custom options, particularly around trust anchors or certificate validity if needed.

An example initialization of a Linkerd installation with mTLS configuration:

```
linkerd install --identity-trust-anchors-file trust.crt \
                --identity-issuer-certificate-file issuer.crt \
                --identity-issuer-key-file issuer.key | kubectl apply -f -
```

This command sets up Linkerd with specific trust anchors and issues certificates necessary for mTLS.

**Observing mTLS Activity:**

Monitoring mTLS activity is crucial to ensuring its correct operation. The status of mTLS can be verified using Linkerd's command-line tools, which provide insights into the mesh's security posture.

The following command will display information about mTLS status across the mesh:

```
linkerd stat --from resource.type/namespace/name
```

Output from this command displays the status of mTLS, including indicators if mTLS is being actively used by services for communication.

**Security Policies and mTLS:**

Beyond enforcing mTLS, Linkerd permits the definition of fine-grained network policies, further strengthening security enforcement. Policies can restrict which services are allowed to communicate at the application layer.

The combination of mTLS and policy-driven traffic control not only secures data exchange but also mitigates risk by narrowing the surface area available to potential attackers.

**Interoperation with Other Systems:**

Linkerd's implementation of mTLS is designed to work seamlessly within a Kubernetes environment, but interoperates effectively with external systems seeking secure and authenticated interactions. It achieves this by allowing the export and import of certificates to and from other trust authorities or PKI systems if such interoperability is required.

**Performance Considerations:**

While encryption offers substantial security benefits, it does come with some performance overhead. Linkerd's design minimizes this impact by optimizing the TLS handshake process and reusing connections wherever feasible. The resulting performance loss is generally negligible and well worth the augmented security posture provided by mTLS.

**Addressing Potential Challenges:**

- **Security Misconfigurations:** A critical concern with encryption systems like mTLS is the potential for security misconfigurations. Linkerd automates nearly all aspects of certificate issuance and management, diminishing the likelihood of human error.

- **Legacy System Compatibility:** Integrating systems that do not support mTLS may pose challenges. Linkerd provides support pathways, such as edge termination, where mTLS can be terminated at service mesh edges, facilitating the use of existing systems with Linkerd security layers.

Linkerd's automatic mTLS encryption feature substantially enhances microservices security. By leveraging automated mutual authentication and encryption, Linkerd provides a foundational security layer that is both robust and operationally efficient, easing the burden on developers and operators. With mTLS, security becomes inherently integrated, allowing for focus on innovating and scaling services confidently within a secure, trusted infrastructure. Run failed with status: expired

## 4.4 Service Latency and Health Checks

Within a microservices architecture, understanding and managing service latency and health are critical for maintaining optimal performance and reliability. Service latency affects user experience directly, while continuous health checks are vital for ensuring that individual services remain operational and available. Linkerd provides comprehensive features to both measure and manage latency, as well as implement robust health checks that maintain the integrity of the services mesh.

**Understanding Service Latency:**

Latency in microservices refers to the time it takes for a request to travel from the client to the server and back. This latency can originate from various sources within a service mesh, including network delay, traffic congestion, processing time, and queue delays. Identifying and managing latency is essential to delivering responsive applications.

Linkerd measures latency by tracking the time interval between the initiation of a request and the reception of its response. This measurement is captured at each hop in the service mesh, providing detailed latency metrics at both the service and route level.

Latency is often expressed in percentiles (P50, P95, P99), representing the distribution of latencies observed over a period. These percentiles help identify common and edge-case latencies affecting user experiences.

**Latency Measurement in Linkerd:**

- Automatic Metrics Collection: Linkerd automatically collects latency metrics for all service communication within the mesh without requiring modification to the service code. This automatic collection facilitates seamless integration into existing workflows, offering instantaneous latency insights.

- Dashboard Visualizations: Collected metrics can be visualized through dashboards, commonly using Grafana, providing a real-time overview of latency trends. Grafana dashboards visualize these temporal patterns, highlighting periods of heightened latency or abnormal behavior, and are invaluable for tracking performance over time.

A Grafana query fetching latency statistics might appear as follows:

```
avg(rate(request_latency_ms_sum[5m])) by (service)
```

This example query calculates the average request latency over the last five minutes for each service, offering tangible insights into real-time performance.

**Health Checks:**

Health checks are a proactive way to ensure service availability within microservices architectures. They monitor service health by performing routine checks on service endpoints to ascertain their operational status. These checks can either be liveness checks to determine if a service is functioning or readiness checks to assess if a service is ready to handle requests.

Linkerd supports both active and passive health checks:

- Active Health Checks: Active health checks involve sending periodic requests to service endpoints to confirm their availability. If a service fails a health check, Linkerd automatically routes traffic away from the problematic instance and attempts to find a

## 4.4. SERVICE LATENCY AND HEALTH CHECKS

healthy one. Active checks require explicit configuration within services.

Example configuration for active health checks:

```
readinessProbe:
  httpGet:
    path: /healthz
    port: 8080
  initialDelaySeconds: 5
  periodSeconds: 10
  timeoutSeconds: 2
```

In this configuration, the service is checked every 10 seconds with a request to the '/healthz' endpoint, asserting that the service is ready and accepting connections.

- Passive Health Checks: Passive health checks, or circuit breakers, are implemented directly within Linkerd's data plane, monitoring the success and failure of incoming requests. If requests consistently fail, Linkerd may reduce traffic sent to the offending service instance, allowing it time to recover.

The passive check mechanism integrates seamlessly with Linkerd's load balancing, automatically reacting to observed failures without additional configuration overhead.

**Advanced Latency Management:**

Linkerd enables advanced latency management strategies, including retry logic, timeouts, and traffic shaping, to enhance overall application performance and stability:

- Retries: By enabling retries, Linkerd can automatically attempt failed requests multiple times before returning an error, which can mitigate transient issues. The retry strategy in Linkerd is adjustable to minimize unnecessary retries and manage network strain.

- Timeouts: Configuring timeouts establishes the maximum duration Linkerd will wait for a service to respond. If a response is not received within this window, the request times out, preventing client-side delays. Timeouts vary per route and service, tailored to individual service SLAs.

Configuring timeout settings in Linkerd:

```
apiVersion: linkerd.io/v1beta2
kind: ServiceProfile
metadata:
  name: service-name.domain.svc.cluster.local
spec:
  routes:
  - name: /routePath
    timeout: "200ms"
```

Through this configuration, requests routed to '/routePath' will timeout if not completed within 200 milliseconds.

- Traffic Shaping: Traffic shaping helps manage how requests are distributed across services to minimize latency. By implementing priority-based routing, Linkerd can prioritize critical paths, ensuring high-priority requests experience reduced latencies.

**Latency and Health Monitoring Tools in Linkerd:**

Enhancing these capabilities, Linkerd's CLI provides direct means to query latency and health metrics, offering comprehensive insight without the need for third-party integrations. The 'linkerd stat' command outputs a summary of latency and health status at varying levels of granularity:

```
linkerd stat deploy --namespace=default
```

The output displays the P50, P95, and P99 latencies for specified deployments, enabling rapid identification of latency anomalies.

**Proactive Maintenance and Optimization:**

Regular monitoring of service latency and health enables identification of trends and potential bottlenecks before they impair user experiences. Using historical data, teams can preemptively optimize code pathways, scale resources, refine dependency management, or enhance service implementation strategies.

Through proactive maintenance plans based on latency and health insights, services can achieve their performance goals consistently, adapt to changes in demand, and maintain user satisfaction.

**Integrating AI/ML for Predictive Analysis:**

Leveraging machine learning (ML) models within Linkerd's observability stack accounts for predictive analysis, automating trend detection and aiding forecasting. By integrating ML frameworks and processing telemetry data, organizations can predict latency performance shifts, project load requirements, and plan infrastructure expansion in advance.

Service latency management and health checks in Linkerd lay the groundwork for a resilient microservices ecosystem. By prioritizing robust monitoring and management strategies, organizations gain the capacity to deliver trustable, scalable, and user-centric services whilst continually refining their operational architecture. Through its blend of automatic metrics, intelligent load balancing, and failover capabilities, Linkerd strengthens service reliability, preparing infrastructure to meet the demands of modern architectures.

## 4.5 Advanced Traffic Control

Traffic control within a microservices infrastructure encompasses strategies and mechanisms that manage how requests are routed, prioritized, and handled across distributed service instances. In complex architectures, advanced traffic control is essential for ensuring that service delivery remains consistent, efficient, and aligned with organizational requirements. Linkerd, as a robust service mesh solution, offers extensive features for implementing advanced traffic control, facilitating granular management over service interactions.

Linkerd implements advanced traffic control by enabling policies and configurations that guide how traffic traverses the mesh. This control extends beyond simple load balancing and routing, incorporating sophisticated mechanisms such as traffic splitting, request routing rules, service rate limiting, fault injection, and dynamic policies tailored to meet specific needs.

**Traffic Splitting:**

Traffic splitting refers to the distribution of incoming service requests across different service versions or instances based on predefined rules. This mechanism is integral to progressive delivery strategies like canary deployments, where new service versions are introduced with minimal risk.

Linkerd's traffic splitting capability enables users to direct a percentage of user traffic to alternate service implementations, allowing for testing in production with controlled exposure. This is configured through Service Mesh Interface (SMI) TrafficSplit resources which define the main service and its backends, along with the proportional distribution of traffic.

Example configuration of a TrafficSplit resource:

```
apiVersion: split.smi-spec.io/v1alpha3
kind: TrafficSplit
metadata:
  name: example-split
spec:
  service: my-app
  backends:
  - service: my-app-v1
    weight: 80
  - service: my-app-v2
    weight: 20
```

In this configuration, 'my-app' is logically split between 'my-app-v1' and 'my-app-v2', allocating 80% traffic to the former and 20% to the latter.

**Request Routing Rules:**

Linkerd provides the ability to define request routing rules, managing which service endpoints handle specific request types. This feature empowers users to direct traffic conditionally based on attributes like the request path, HTTP methods, headers, and more.

These route rules are established in Service Profiles and can be matched to any route attributes. Incorporating routing rules provides sophisticated mechanisms for API versioning, A/B testing, and backward compatibility scenarios.

Here's an example ServiceProfile with conditional routing based on HTTP request path:

```
apiVersion: linkerd.io/v1alpha2
kind: ServiceProfile
metadata:
  name: my-service
spec:
  routes:
  - name: GET /api/v1/users
```

## 4.5. ADVANCED TRAFFIC CONTROL

```
    condition:
      method: GET
      pathRegex: /api/v1/users
    retryBudget:
      retryRatio: 0.2
      ttl: 10s
      minRetriesPerSecond: 10
  - name: POST /api/v1/order
    condition:
      method: POST
      pathRegex: /api/v1/order
```

This configuration splits routes based on API endpoints, allowing for individualized rule applications such as retry policies per route.

**Service Rate Limiting:**

Limiting request rates to services ensures that instances are not overwhelmed by excessive traffic, protecting upstream services and data stores from potential degradation. Linkerd allows defining rate limiting policies at multiple levels based on route metrics. While natively Linkerd doesn't define rate limiting mechanisms within its configurations, integrating external systems such as NGINX or using third-party proxies like Envoy alongside Linkerd can facilitate rate limiting.

Example rate limiting setup using Envoy alongside Linkerd might involve configuring Envoy's rate limiting service:

```
domain: my-service
descriptors:
  - key: generic_key
    value: rate_limit
    rate_limit:
      unit: minute
      requests_per_unit: 100
```

**Fault Injection:**

Testing the resilience of services against failures is crucial for predicting service behavior under duress. Fault injection is a strategy where artificial faults are introduced to assess how systems cope with errors.

Linkerd can be leveraged alongside tools like chaos engineering frameworks to execute fault injection, examining services for fault tolerance and robustness systematically.

Fault scenarios might include response delay injections, network packet drops, or request errors, testing the system's ability to maintain operational integrity.

**Dynamic Traffic Policies:**

Dynamic traffic policies allow for real-time adjustments based on current service conditions and metrics. Linkerd's observability and smart routing capabilities provide means to develop dynamic policies that react to traffic patterns, anomalies, or environmental changes without manual intervention.

For instance, traffic policies can dynamically engage congestion control when traffic exceeds predefined levels, modifying load balancing strategies to accommodate increased demand without service performance deterioration.

Enabling such policies involves a combination of monitoring and alerting, leveraging Prometheus metrics, and orchestrating responses through Linkerd and supplementary tooling.

**Integrating Policies for Comprehensive Control:**

Comprehensive management of traffic requires a coherent strategy that combines multiple traffic control methodologies. By integrating advanced traffic control capabilities, organizations can formulate policies that capture desired behaviors across a range of scenarios, unifying control under Linkerd's service mesh architecture.

Consider integrating policies for high availability scenarios: traffic splitting can act to disseminate load, routing rules can ensure appropriate handlers manage requests while rate limits protect system stability, woven with planned fallback routes during contingencies.

**Demonstrating Application Agility:**

Advanced traffic control underpins application agility, allowing for rapid adaptations to shifting conditions:

- **Autonomous Scaling:** Application instances may be dynamically scaled to handle increased loads discovered through observing real-time traffic patterns.

- **Efficient Resource Utilization:** Traffic management aligns service requests with resource availability, ensuring optimal use of computational resources.

## 4.5. ADVANCED TRAFFIC CONTROL

- **High-velocity Deployment:** Progressive delivery techniques enabled by traffic splitting and gating manage risk during code rollouts and upgrades.

**Case Studies and Use Scenarios:**

To further emphasize the importance of advanced traffic control, consider real-world scenarios where these capabilities generate profound business value:

- **E-commerce Traffic Surge Mitigation:** During promotional events, precise traffic control ensures stability, directing users overperforming service versions or untested beta functionality deemed risk-mitigating.

- **Multitenancy Management:** Balancing traffic between tenant services, privileging higher-tier tenants with reduced latency access, ensures fair and SLA-compliant resource distribution.

- **Incident Remediation:** Fast-paced analysis of fault domains during incidents allows for routing around defective services, minimizing downtime and safeguarding the overall user experience through vigilant route cordoning.

These scenarios underscore the importance and versatility of advanced traffic control methods available within Linkerd's service mesh, showcasing how they drive business success by increasing systems' resilience, flexibility, and preparedness to handle contemporary application demands.

Advanced traffic control strategies provided by Linkerd equip organizations with tools necessary to navigate the complexities of modern service demands. Through proactive traffic shaping and precise control, service mesh participants experience enhanced reliability, agility, and maintained end-user satisfaction, ultimately embodying a forward-thinking approach to service architecture management.

# Chapter 5

# Securing Services with Linkerd

Linkerd provides comprehensive security solutions to safeguard service-to-service communications within a microservices architecture. This chapter details the implementation of mutual TLS (mTLS) to ensure encrypted connections, thus maintaining data integrity and confidentiality. It also covers identity management and network policies for enforcing robust security controls. Additionally, the chapter discusses certificate management practices, including automated rotation, and techniques for auditing and monitoring to detect and respond to potential threats. By leveraging these security features, users can protect their applications from common vulnerabilities and unauthorized access.

## 5.1 Understanding mTLS in Linkerd

In microservices architecture, secure communication between services is paramount to safeguard against unauthorized data access and interception. Linkerd, as a service mesh, provides a robust mechanism for securing communication between services using mutual TLS (mTLS).

This concept is crucial in establishing trust and encryption across service interactions within the mesh, ensuring both confidentiality and integrity.

Mutual TLS, an extension of the standard Transport Layer Security protocol, facilitates authentication between client and server in both directions. In a typical TLS handshake, only the server is authenticated by the client. However, mTLS strengthens this by requiring both client and server to authenticate each other using their respective digital certificates. This bidirectional authentication is pivotal in microservices ecosystems, where multiple services must securely interact with one another.

Linkerd leverages a sidecar proxy model, which implicitly handles secure communication without requiring modifications to the application code. Each service instance is paired with a Linkerd proxy, which intercepts and manages traffic between the respective services.

The mTLS strategy is implemented at the proxy level by encrypting the traffic between the proxies of the interacting services. This ensures that data travels securely over the network, with link encryption and server authentication as fundamental components. The Linkerd control plane manages the distribution and lifecycle of certificates used for mTLS, ensuring that each proxy receives a cryptographically secure identity. This identity is used when establishing mTLS connections.

The core architecture of Linkerd beginning with the mTLS setup involves several key components:

- **Identity Service:** This component issues short-lived certificates for service identity, ensuring frequent rotation and reducing the risk of compromise.

- **Certificate Authority (CA):** At the heart of Linkerd's security, the CA vouches for the authenticity of identity certificates, signing them with a root certificate.

- **Proxies:** These facilitate transparent service communication, handling mTLS handshakes on behalf of the services.

The mTLS handshake process in Linkerd is integral to securing communication channels within the service mesh. Upon initiating a con-

## 5.1. UNDERSTANDING MTLS IN LINKERD

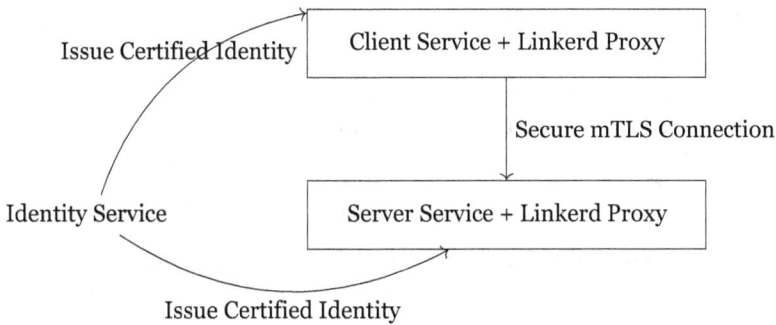

Figure 5.1: mTLS Architecture in Linkerd

nection, the client and server proxies engage in a series of exchanges to authenticate each other's identity, as depicted in the diagram.

The detailed steps of the mTLS handshake include:

- **ClientHello Message:** The client proxy sends this message to indicate its intention to communicate with the server, including supported cryptographic algorithms.

- **ServerHello Message:** The server proxy responds, choosing a mutually agreeable algorithm and providing its certificate for authentication.

- **Client Certificate Request:** As part of mutual authentication, the server requests the client's certificate.

- **Certificate Verification:** Both client and server verify each other's certificates against trusted certificate authorities.

- **Session Key Exchange:** Secure session keys are derived and exchanged to encrypt the communication channel.

```
Client: --> ClientHello
Server: <-- ServerHello
        <-- CertificateRequest from Server
Client: --> Certificate
Client: --> Finished
Server: <-- Finished
        --> Encrypted Data Transmission
```

Utilizing mTLS within Linkerd affords numerous security advantages:

- **Data Confidentiality:** Encryption of data in transit renders it unreadable to unauthorized entities.
- **Service Authentication:** Mutual authentication prevents untrusted services from masquerading as legitimate ones.
- **Data Integrity:** The cryptographic techniques ensure that data is neither altered nor tampered with during transmission.

The architecture's ability to auto-inject the Linkerd proxy simplifies the integration of mTLS, allowing applications to benefit from enhanced security with minimal interference. Moreover, the automatic certificate rotation further strengthens security by reducing the exposure window for any compromised credentials.

Configuring mTLS within a Linkerd deployment involves concise, well-defined steps. Admins need to ensure that the control plane is appropriately set up to distribute identity certificates, and that proxies can communicate effectively with one another.

The configuration process typically involves:

- Launching the Linkerd CLI to install the control plane and inject the proxies.
- Ensuring each service has the Linkerd proxy sidecar injected.

Example of injecting Linkerd into a Kubernetes deployment:

```
kubectl get deploy -n mynamespace -o yaml \
| linkerd inject - \
| kubectl apply -f -
```

Upon completion, Linkerd will begin managing mTLS connections automatically. The congenital setup coupled with monitoring ensures that any security anomalies can be promptly detected and addressed. Through the Linkerd dashboard or via CLI commands, users can observe the status of mTLS connections, effectively managing their deployment's security posture.

For example, monitoring mTLS status:

## 5.1. UNDERSTANDING MTLS IN LINKERD

```
linkerd stat deploy --from deploy --to deploy
```

The output of such a command provides detailed insights into the encrypted communication status, assisting in maintaining system integrity.

```
NAMESPACE     NAME        MESHED   SUCCESS    RPS   LATENCY_P50 ...
mynamespace   myservice1  2/2      97.5%      0.5   29ms
mynamespace   myservice2  2/2      100.0%     0.1   21ms
...
```

Advanced configurations in Linkerd for mTLS allow for more refined control over security policies and encryption parameters. For instance, setting strict validation modes or customizing the cipher suites utilized can enhance security according to specific needs.

Adapting mTLS to various cybersecurity policies can also involve adjusting trust anchors used by the service mesh for verifying certificates. Trust anchors are typically configured during the bootstrap phase of the Linkerd control plane but can be modified as requirements evolve.

Furthermore, the integration of additional tools like Prometheus and Grafana can enrich the monitoring and management of mTLS connections. Through precise dashboards, security administrators can track certificate expiry, handshake failures, or unusual data patterns that might indicate an attempted compromise.

To customize trust roots:

```
linkerd install --identity-trust-anchors-file ./ca.crt \
--identity-issuer-certificate-file ./issuer.crt \
--identity-issuer-key-file ./issuer.key | kubectl apply -f -
```

This setup helps tailor mTLS configurations to an organization's unique demands, extending security beyond default settings and providing a comprehensive security mesh layer.

The development and maintenance of secure service-to-service communication channels are fundamental when managing modern application architectures. By leveraging Linkerd's robust approach to implementing mTLS, developers and system administrators can ensure that their microservices environments remain resilient against potential threats, thereby guaranteeing both data privacy and trustworthiness across the system.

## 5.2 Identity Management and Security Policies

In distributed systems architecture, such as microservices environments, the management of identities and the enforcement of security policies are vital components in securing service-to-service interactions. This section delves into how Linkerd manages identity within its service mesh and the crucial role security policies play in enhancing the integrity and confidentiality of communications between services.

Identity management in Linkerd revolves around the core principle of establishing an authenticated identity for each service within the mesh. This mechanism ensures that any communication within the service mesh is validated for authenticity, thus preventing unauthorized access attempts. Central to this process is the use of cryptographic certificates issued to services, identifying them uniquely within the mesh.

Linkerd implements its identity management through a dynamic and secure certificate issuance process. The identity service component within Linkerd's control plane is responsible for managing these certificates, which are pivotal in facilitating mutual TLS (mTLS) connections across the mesh. The identity framework in Linkerd relies on several key elements:

- **Service Identity:** Each service in the mesh has a distinct identity that is represented by a service account. The identity is tied to a short-lived certificate that the service uses to authenticate itself.

- **Identity Controller:** Deployed as part of the control plane, this component is responsible for issuing and rotating certificates. It communicates with a Certificate Authority (CA) to sign certificate requests and ensure the secure validation of identities.

- **Certificate Lifecycle Management:** Certificates in Linkerd are short-lived, typically between hours to days, which inherently enhances security by minimizing the risk of misuse.

The identity allocation process begins with the deployment of the control plane and persists as long as the service mesh is operational. Let's

## 5.2. IDENTITY MANAGEMENT AND SECURITY POLICIES

explore this process further:

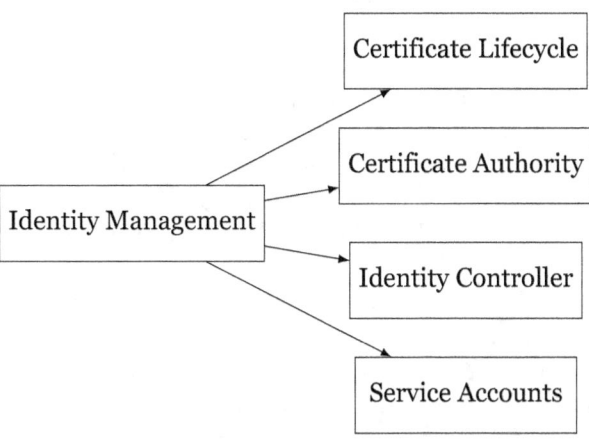

Figure 5.2: Components of Identity Management in Linkerd

A detailed understanding of the certificate issuance and rotation process is essential for ensuring seamless integration and management of service identities:

- **Initialization:**
    - Upon service deployment, a service account is created within the Kubernetes ecosystem, which Linkerd utilizes to establish initial identity credentials.

- **Certificate Signing Request (CSR):**
    - The service, via its Linkerd proxy, generates a CSR and sends it to the identity controller.

- **Verification and Signing:**
    - The identity controller verifies the CSR against the service's credentials and communicates with the CA to receive a signed certificate.

- **Certificate Distribution:**

- The signed certificate is then distributed back to the service proxy, which uses it to establish mTLS connections.

- **Automated Rotation:**
  - The certificates are designed to be short-lived. Linkerd automates the renewal process by initiating a new CSR well before the expiration of the current certificate.

Below is an example script demonstrating a typical certificate handling scenario:

```bash
#!/bin/bash

# Kubernetes namespace
NAMESPACE=mynamespace

# Generate a new Certificate Signing Request
CSR_NAME=my-csr
kubectl create csr $CSR_NAME \
  --namespace=$NAMESPACE \
  --request-crt-file=cert.csr \
  --output=jsonpath='{.status.certificate}' | base64 --decode

# Approve the CSR
kubectl certificate approve $CSR_NAME -n $NAMESPACE

# Retrieve the signed certificate
kubectl get csr $CSR_NAME -o jsonpath='{.status.certificate}' | base64 --decode > signed-cert.crt
```

This script outlines how a CSR is generated and signed, a process that occurs transparently within Linkerd's service mesh but can also be administered manually for explicit control over security setups.

Security policies in Linkerd are designed to govern service interactions and ensure adherence to predefined security standards. These policies enhance the security and robustness of the service mesh by preventing unauthorized access and enforcing communication protocols.

Security policies encompass various aspects, including:

- **Network Policies:** Define which services can communicate, enabling traffic control between specific services or across namespaces.

- **Access Policies:** Control access rights to various services, protecting data and functionality from unauthorized modification.

## 5.2. IDENTITY MANAGEMENT AND SECURITY POLICIES

Network policies in Linkerd are employed to regulate traffic flows, ensuring that services can only communicate with permitted peers. Kubernetes NetworkPolicies can be used alongside Linkerd to define permissible connectivity.

For example, the following YAML manifest illustrates a basic network policy restricting incoming traffic to only allow communication from specific pods:

```
apiVersion: networking.k8s.io/v1
kind: NetworkPolicy
metadata:
  name: allow-specific-pods
  namespace: mynamespace
spec:
  podSelector:
    matchLabels:
      role: backend
  ingress:
  - from:
    - podSelector:
        matchLabels:
          access: allowed
  policyTypes:
  - Ingress
```

This policy ensures that only pods labeled with access: allowed are permitted to send traffic to pods with the role: backend label, thereby tightening network security within the mesh.

Role-Based Access Control (RBAC) plays a substantial role in managing who can access or perform actions within the Linkerd environment. It categorizes permissions based on roles rather than individuals, maintaining a structured security approach.

Example of configuring RBAC for managing service access:

```
apiVersion: rbac.authorization.k8s.io/v1
kind: Role
metadata:
  namespace: mynamespace
  name: access-manager
rules:
- apiGroups: [""]
  resources: ["pods", "services"]
  verbs: ["get", "list", "watch"]

---

apiVersion: rbac.authorization.k8s.io/v1
kind: RoleBinding
metadata:
```

```
  name: bind-access-manager
  namespace: mynamespace
subjects:
- kind: User
  name: service-user
  apiGroup: rbac.authorization.k8s.io
roleRef:
  kind: Role
  name: access-manager
  apiGroup: rbac.authorization.k8s.io
```

In this configuration, a Role is defined with permissions to perform certain actions on resources, such as get, list, and watch, only within the mynamespace. It is then attached to a specific User via a RoleBinding, granting that user the defined permissions.

Implementing effective identity and access management rewards organizations with enhanced security and operational resilience. Some of the best practices in managing identities and securing policies within Linkerd include:

- **Principle of Least Privilege:** Always assign the minimum set of permissions necessary for a service or user to function, reducing the potential impact of a security breach.

- **Regular Audits and Monitoring:** Continuously monitor and review access patterns to detect anomalies. Use Linkerd's observability features to track mTLS connection statuses and network traffic.

- **Comprehensive Documentation:** Keep thorough documentation of access policies and identity management changes, aiding in transparency and compliance audits.

- **Automation and CI/CD Integration:** Automate identity and security policy deployment in CI/CD pipelines, ensuring consistent application throughout environments and diminishing manual errors.

With restorative features such as visual analytics and detailed metrics, Linkerd allows teams to quickly adopt and enforce identity and security policies systematically. These elements are indispensable in maintaining the security, integrity, and efficiency of dynamic service meshes like those implemented by Linkerd in Kubernetes. As organizations acclimate to these sophisticated systems, adherence to security protocols becomes a paramount facet of service mesh deployment and management.

## 5.3 Configuring Network Policies

Network policies in a Kubernetes environment are critical for controlling the traffic flow between pods and ensuring isolation within a cluster. In a service mesh like Linkerd, configuring network policies involves setting rules that dictate permissible communication pathways between services, thus enhancing security, compliance, and operational stability. This section delves into the intricacies of configuring network policies tailored to environments utilizing Linkerd, focusing on both foundational concepts and advanced configuration techniques.

**Understanding Network Policies** Network policies are essentially a set of rules that specify how pods in a Kubernetes cluster can communicate with each other and with other network endpoints. These policies enable administrators to control traffic at the IP level, governing both ingress (incoming) and egress (outgoing) traffic to and from the pods. By default, pods in Kubernetes can communicate freely, thus network policies are used to restrict this communication to only what is necessary.

In the context of a service mesh such as Linkerd, network policies work alongside the mesh's intrinsic traffic control mechanisms to deliver a robust security framework. The introduction of service mesh facilitates the enforcement of network policies with minimal disruption to application development processes.

```
apiVersion: networking.k8s.io/v1
kind: NetworkPolicy
metadata:
  name: default-deny
  namespace: default
spec:
  podSelector: {}
  policyTypes:
  - Ingress
```

In this example, a default deny-all ingress policy is depicted. This policy blocks all incoming traffic unless explicitly allowed by other policies in the same namespace, thereby acting as a fundamental safeguard.

**Implementing Network Policies with Linkerd** Incorporating network policies in a Linkerd-enabled environment involves understanding the relationship between Kubernetes network policy objects and Linkerd's service mesh functionalities. A coherent setup ensures that network traffic preferences align with security and performance goals.

- **Ingress Controls:** Define which services or external clients can initiate communication with your pod. This is particularly useful for publicly exposed services that require strict access control.

- **Egress Controls:** Specify external IPs or services with which pods are permitted to communicate, ensuring fine-grained traffic management and protection against data exfiltration.

Combining these features allows you to effectively manage traffic between the microservices in your system.

```
apiVersion: networking.k8s.io/v1
kind: NetworkPolicy
metadata:
  name: allow-client-to-backend
  namespace: app-namespace
spec:
  podSelector:
    matchLabels:
      role: backend
  policyTypes:
  - Ingress
  - Egress
  ingress:
  - from:
    - podSelector:
        matchLabels:
          role: client
  egress:
  - to:
    - ipBlock:
        cidr: 203.0.113.0/24
    ports:
    - protocol: TCP
      port: 8080
```

## 5.3. CONFIGURING NETWORK POLICIES

In this advanced configuration, ingress traffic is only allowed from pods with the label 'role: client', and egress traffic is restricted to a specific IP range, ensuring restricted data flow both inwards and outwards.

**Utilizing Linkerd for Fine-Grained Traffic Management** Network policies define traffic control at the network layer, whereas Linkerd can provide additional controls at the application layer. The collaboration of both allows users to leverage Linkerd's comprehensive capabilities in service authorization and observability.

Key advantages include:

- **Automatic mTLS Encryption:** Linkerd encrypts all traffic within the service mesh boundary, adding a layer of security regardless of the network policy settings.

- **Traffic Shaping and Routing:** Linkerd enables intelligent traffic routing decisions, such as load balancing and failover handling, without needing to change network policy configurations.

Integrating these features provides powerful control mechanisms over network traffic, supporting both security and high availability.

**Combining Policies for Maximum Protection** For extensive protection and resource optimization, it's advisable to create a suite of network policies that cater to different segments of traffic management (e.g., internal, external, sensitive-disclosure). Here we explore combined policies:

```
apiVersion: networking.k8s.io/v1
kind: NetworkPolicy
metadata:
  name: internal-to-internal
  namespace: financing
spec:
  podSelector:
    matchLabels:
      access: internal
  ingress:
  - from:
    - podSelector:
        matchLabels:
```

```
        access: internal
  policyTypes:
  - Ingress
---
apiVersion: networking.k8s.io/v1
kind: NetworkPolicy
metadata:
  name: external-access
  namespace: public
spec:
  podSelector:
    matchLabels:
      exposure: public
  ingress:
  - from:
    - ipBlock:
        cidr: 0.0.0.0/0
    - namespaceSelector:
        matchLabels:
          access: external-allowed
  policyTypes:
  - Ingress
```

In this configuration, two different network policies illustrate restricting internal communication to specific pods and allowing public access to specific services while limiting permissions.

**Security Best Practices for Implementing Network Policies**
Adopting network policies demands adherence to best practices that ensure the balance between security enforcement and system performance:

- **Layered Security Approach:** Use defense-in-depth strategies; combine network policies with mTLS and application-layer policies.

- **Regular Audits and Validation:** Continuously review policies and conduct audits to ensure compliance with security mandates.

- **Granular Control and Frequent Updates:** Keep policies granular to target specific traffic and update regularly to adapt to evolving network dynamics.

- **Documentation and Automation:** Maintain comprehensive documentation and automate policy deployments to reduce errors and enhance consistency.

## 5.3. CONFIGURING NETWORK POLICIES

These practices, coupled with continuous monitoring, contribute to a more resilient and secure service architecture.

**Policy Testing and Validation** Before applying network policies in a production environment, rigorous testing is required to validate their impact and ensure they behave as intended. Testing can involve:

- **Policy Emulation Tools:** Use emulation tools to simulate network conditions and check how policies interact.

- **Debugging with Linkerd and Kubernetes Tools:** Utilize log tracing, packet capturing, and observability tools to diagnose issues and optimize policies.

An example utility script showcasing testing and validation activities:

```bash
#!/bin/bash

# Test connectivity between two pods in different namespaces
pod1="client-pod"
pod2="backend-pod"
namespace1="client-namespace"
namespace2="backend-namespace"

# Check if the pods can directly communicate over the specified port
kubectl exec -n $namespace1 $pod1 -- nc -vz $pod2.backend-namespace.svc.cluster.
    local 8080

# Output the result
if [ $? -eq 0 ]; then
    echo "Connection successful: Network policy permits traffic."
else
    echo "Connection failed: Network policy restricts traffic."
fi
```

This example checks connectivity policies by attempting direct communication between designated pods and logs the status based on success metrics.

Network policy configuration, when correctly applied with Linkerd's service mesh capabilities, equips systems with powerful tools for securing microservices. Continuous review and refinement of these policies are essential in maintaining a robust security posture in rapidly evolving environments. The synthesis of network policy configurations with mTLS and application-layer traffic management provides a substantial defense mechanism, ensuring that communication channels are efficiently secure against potential intrusion.

## 5.4 Certificate Management and Rotation

In a microservices architecture facilitated by a service mesh like Linkerd, the management of SSL/TLS certificates is crucial for the security of service-to-service communication. Certificates authenticate identities, encrypt traffic, and ensure data integrity as it moves through the network. This section addresses the robust mechanisms Linkerd provides for certificate management and the critical processes of automated certificate rotation which minimize the risk of credential compromise.

Certificate management in a service mesh involves generating, distributing, validating, and renewing certificates. These certificates underpin mutual TLS (mTLS) connections, securing the data exchanges between microservices. Effective management ensures that these cryptographic tokens are current, valid, and securely handled throughout their lifecycle.

- **Certificate Authority (CA):** The CA is responsible for issuing and signing certificates. It forms the trust root of the Linkerd mesh by validating identity requests from service proxies.

- **Identity Controller:** Part of Linkerd's control plane, this component manages certificate requests and rotations, ensuring identity certificates are always up-to-date.

- **Linkerd Proxies:** Each service instance runs alongside a Linkerd proxy which uses these certificates to authenticate and encrypt connections with peer proxies.

The combined operation of these components ensures a secure and seamless distribution of identity to services within a Linkerd deployment. A typical communication flow involves the following steps:

1. The Linkerd proxy generates a Certificate Signing Request (CSR).
2. The identity controller verifies the CSR and forwards it to the CA.
3. The CA signs the certificate and sends it back through the identity controller to the originating proxy.
4. The proxy receives the signed certificate and uses it to establish mTLS connections.

**Automated Certificate Rotation**

A cornerstone of Linkerd's certificate management system is automated certificate rotation, a necessary process to mitigate the risks of certificate expiration and unauthorized exposure. Regular rotation reduces the window in which a compromised certificate can be abused if obtained by malicious entities.

Automated rotation involves the following:

- **Short-Lived Certificates:** Certificates are configured with short lifetimes, often hours to days, emphasizing regularly scheduled renewals.

- **Proactive Renewal:** The Linkerd identity controller proactively generates new CSRs well before certificates expire, ensuring a seamless transition between old and new certificates.

- **Zero-Downtime Deployment:** The rotation is carried out in a manner that prevents connection drops, preserving the stability and reliability of service interactions.

```
# Examine the current certificate's expiration
kubectl get secret linkerd-identity-issuer -n linkerd -o yaml

# Trigger manual certificate rotation if needed
linkerd upgrade --identity-issuer-certificate-file=path/to/new-cert.crt \
--identity-issuer-key-file=path/to/new-key.key | kubectl apply -f -
```

This sequence illustrates how to inspect certificate details and perform manual rotations—although Linkerd automates this process, understanding the manual procedure is critical for troubleshooting or policy updates.

## Ensuring Security in Certificate Management

Effective certificate management must adhere to security best practices to protect against potential vulnerabilities:

- **Regular Audits:** Constant audits and verifications of certificate deployment can help identify and swiftly resolve discrepancies or breaches.

- **Secure Storage:** Private keys and certificates must be stored securely using mechanisms like Kubernetes Secrets or HashiCorp Vault to prevent unauthorized access.

- **Access Control Policies:** Ensure that only authorized entities have the ability to request or renew certificates, reducing the attack surface.

## Handling Expired and Compromised Certificates

Managing expired or compromised certificates entails swift action to prevent disruptions or security violations. With Linkerd, this process is streamlined to restore secure communication effectively:

1. **Detection:** Utilize monitoring and alerting systems to identify when certificates are close to expiration or suspected to be compromised.

2. **Revocation and Renewal:** In Linkerd, this is largely automated. Upon detection of an expired certificate, the system self-heals by issuing a new certificate without manual intervention.

3. **Deployment and Validation:** The newly issued certificate is deployed across service proxies, with tests conducted to confirm successful handovers.

```
apiVersion: v1
data:
  tls.crt: ...
  tls.key: ...
kind: Secret
metadata:
  name: linkerd-identity-issuer
  namespace: linkerd
type: kubernetes.io/tls
```

## 5.4. CERTIFICATE MANAGEMENT AND ROTATION

```yaml
---
apiVersion: cert-manager.io/v1
kind: Certificate
metadata:
  name: issuer-cert
  namespace: linkerd
spec:
  secretName: linkerd-identity-issuer
  issuerRef:
    name: linkerd-ca
    kind: ClusterIssuer
```

This YAML snippet demonstrates the harnessing of Kubernetes secrets and Cert-Manager to automate certificate issuance and renewal, fitting seamlessly into the Linkerd workflow.

### Monitoring Certificate Health

Regular monitoring of certificate health and validity is critical to maintaining an operational and secure mesh environment. Employing tools such as Cert-Manager, Prometheus, and Grafana provides comprehensive insights into certificate status.

Key monitoring activities include:

- **Expiration Alerts:** Set up alerts to notify system operators well before certificate expiration, allowing time for preemptive actions.

- **Validity Checks:** Continuous validation ensures that certificates in use are legitimate and correctly applied.

- **Proactive Revocation Checks:** Regularly assess the need to revoke certificates due to misuse, non-compliance, or emerging threats.

Example of configuring Prometheus for monitoring certificate expiration:

```yaml
groups:
- name: certificate-expiration.rules
  rules:
  - alert: CertificateExpiringSoon
    expr: time() > kube_secret_tls_cert_not_after{namespace="linkerd"} - 86400
    for: 1h
    labels:
      severity: warning
    annotations:
```

```
summary: "Certificate Expiring Soon"
description: "The certificate for Linkerd is expiring in less than 1 day."
```

This configuration alerts when certificates approach expiration, with a threshold set to trigger a notification a day in advance, providing a buffer period for resolutions.

**Certificate Management Best Practices**

The success of certificate management heavily relies on following best practices that drive security, efficiency, and compliance:

- **Implement Redundancy:** Ensure there are backup methods for certificate issuance and renewal in the event of a CA failure or connectivity issues.
- **Encrypt Traffic:** Consistently use the latest TLS protocols and cipher suites to keep data transmission secure.
- **Educate Team Members:** Train operational and development teams on the importance of certificate management and the potential impacts of negligence.

Adherence to these practices in conjunction with Linkerd's automated processes enables organizations to maintain a confident security stance within their service mesh.

A robust certificate management strategy with seamless rotation is vital to uphold the security and reliability of service-to-service communication within a microservices architecture. Through diligent monitoring and adherence to best practices, organizations ensure secure, efficient operation and mitigate the risks of certificate-related failures or security breaches. Linkerd, with its powerful management capabilities, empowers teams to embed these practices effortlessly into their daily operations, fostering an environment of trust, resilience, and compliance.

## 5.5 Auditing and Security Monitoring

Effective auditing and security monitoring are foundational to maintaining the integrity and resilience of microservices architectures.

## 5.5. AUDITING AND SECURITY MONITORING

Within a service mesh enabled by Linkerd, these processes become even more crucial as microservice interactions proliferate. Systematically capturing and analyzing data related to service communication enables organizations to swiftly detect anomalies, respond to security threats, and ensure compliance with regulatory standards.

Auditing in Linkerd involves collecting comprehensive logs and metrics from service interactions within the mesh, offering visibility into the system's operations. Meanwhile, security monitoring extends this through active oversight of network traffic and behavior, using advanced tools and real-time analytics to safeguard against intrusions and breaches.

Auditing serves multiple roles in securing a microservices environment, primarily focusing on accountability, compliance, and fraud detection. It encompasses the documentation of access controls, service communications, and data flows to provide thorough records that can be reviewed during security investigations or compliance assessments.

Key auditing activities include:

- Access Logging: Monitoring who accesses services, from where, and when, which is crucial for identifying unauthorized access attempts.

- Traffic Analysis: Inspecting network traffic patterns to detect abnormal behaviors or access vectors that could indicate compromised services.

- Change Tracking: Capturing and reporting on changes to configurations and policies, ensuring all modifications are recorded for accountability.

Linkerd enhances auditing through its innate ability to gather detailed telemetry data from within the service mesh. This data provides a rich resource for analyzing service behavior and diagnosing potential issues.

Examples of Linkerd's auditing capabilities:

1. Request and Response Logging: Comprehensive records of service-to-service requests and responses.

2. Policy Enforcement Reporting: Logging of policy applications and related outcomes, indicating whether policies are being adhered to.

3. End-to-End Traffic Tracing: Using tools like OpenTelemetry to trace communications across services, allowing detailed analysis of data paths and communication delays.

Set up example for request logging:

```
# Enable logging on all service requests
kubectl annotate ns default config.linkerd.io/proxy-log-level=linkerd=debug
# Retrieve logs from the Linkerd proxy sidecar
kubectl logs -n default $(kubectl get pod -l app=your-app -o jsonpath='{.items[0].metadata.name}') -c linkerd-proxy
```

Logging setup like this provides detailed insights into how services interact, which is vital for maintaining a robust security posture.

While auditing logs past events, security monitoring is an ongoing process that actively supervises service behavior and network traffic to proactively hunt and respond to anomalies. In a service mesh, monitoring focuses on traffic flows, latency metrics, and error rates that can reveal underlying security vulnerabilities.

Linkerd integrates with popular monitoring and visualization tools, typically Prometheus and Grafana, to offer a graphical user interface and alerting capabilities. Combined, they provide powerful platforms for tracking real-time telemetry data and defining alert parameters for unexpected activity.

Example configuration for using Prometheus with Linkerd:

```
apiVersion: v1
kind: ConfigMap
metadata:
  name: prometheus-config
  namespace: monitoring
data:
  prometheus.yml: |
    global:
      scrape_interval: 15s
    scrape_configs:
    - job_name: 'linkerd'
      static_configs:
      - targets: ['linkerd-proxy:4191']
    alerting:
      alertmanagers:
      - static_configs:
```

## 5.5. AUDITING AND SECURITY MONITORING

```
- targets:
  - 'alertmanager:9093'
```

Examples of metrics to monitor include:

- Latency Metrics: Keeping tabs on request latency can unearth performance bottlenecks or potential denial-of-service attacks.

- Traffic Volume: Sudden spikes or drops in traffic can signal misconfiguration, security breaches, or application failures.

- Error Rates: Monitoring HTTP 4xx/5xx codes helps identify failed requests, misrouted traffic, or unauthorized access attempts.

Beyond basic monitoring, Linkerd can support advanced techniques to detect and mitigate security threats. Applying machine learning models on top of aggregated telemetry data enables the identification of abnormal patterns indicative of cyber threats or misuse.

1. Anomaly Detection: Utilizing unsupervised learning methods like clustering algorithms to identify deviations from established traffic patterns.

2. Behavioral Analysis: Employing signature-based or heuristic algorithms which recognize known malicious behaviors or novel attack vectors.

3. Threat Intelligence Integration: Enriching monitoring data by correlating with external threat intelligence sources to uncover emerging threats.

These techniques represent a holistic approach to identifying and defending against security threats, ensuring microservices are capable of resisting sophisticated attacks.

Effective security monitoring uses alerts to inform stakeholders of critical incidents or potential vulnerabilities, prompting timely responses. Incorporating incident response mechanisms ensures swift mitigation actions and minimizes operational disruptions.

Example of Grafana Alerting Implementation:

```
{
  "id": 1,
  "dashboardId": 1,
  "panelId": 2,
  "name": "High Error Rate",
  "interval": "10s",
  "conditions": [
    {
      "type": "gt",
      "params": [ "5" ],
      "operator": {
        "type": "and"
      },
      "query": {
        "params": [ "A", "5m", "now" ]
      }
    }
  ],
  "actions": [
    {
      "type": "email",
      "settings": {
        "addresses": "team@company.com"
      }
    }
  ],
  "noDataState": "no_data",
  "executionErrorState": "alerting"
}
```

This configuration exemplifies how alerts are set up in Grafana, triggering notifications when error rates exceed a threshold, indicating potential failure conditions or security issues.

Beyond detecting threats, maintaining compliance with industry standards and regulations is essential for enterprises leveraging service meshes like Linkerd. Detailed audit trails coupled with rigorous monitoring support adherence to frameworks like GDPR, HIPAA, and PCI DSS.

- Access Audits: Maintain audit records of system access, ensuring only authorized users and services can interface with sensitive data.

- Data Residency: Monitor service interactions to ensure they comply with data residency requirements, such as storing and processing data within specific geographic boundaries.

- Policy Enforcement Validation: Regularly review security policies and monitoring configurations to align with changing regulatory demands.

Embedding compliance into the security monitoring framework not only aids in avoiding regulatory infractions but also strengthens privacy and data protection strategies enterprise-wide.

Overall, auditing and security monitoring in a Linkerd environment create a security-minded microservices architecture that detects intrusions, complies with regulations, and enhances operational resilience. By maintaining vigilant oversight over service interactions and network traffic, organizations can implement an informed, proactive defense against security threats, ensuring the continuous deployment of services in a safe, compliant, and efficient manner.

## 5.6 Handling External Threats

Securing microservices in a service mesh like Linkerd involves a profound understanding and handling of external threats that can jeopardize the integrity, confidentiality, and availability of microservices. External threats can originate from various sources, including malicious actors exploiting vulnerabilities or misconfigurations inadvertently exposed by developers. Addressing these threats necessitates a comprehensive strategy that incorporates intrusion prevention, threat detection, risk assessment, and response capabilities.

To robustly defend against external threats, it's essential to first classify and understand their nature:

- **DDoS Attacks:** Distributed Denial of Service attacks involve overwhelming services with excessive requests, leading to resource exhaustion and disruptions.

- **Man-in-the-Middle Attacks:** Such attacks intercept communication channels between services, endangering data integrity and confidentiality.

- **Exploitation of Vulnerabilities:** Attackers may exploit known or zero-day vulnerabilities within service components or the underlying infrastructure.

- **Phishing and Social Engineering:** Attempting to gain unauthorized access by manipulating users into revealing credentials or executing malicious commands.

Understanding these threats is paramount in designing appropriate security frameworks and implementing effective countermeasures within Linkerd.

Linkerd offers various tools and integrated practices to fortify microservices against external threats. These strategies include:

- **Mutual TLS (mTLS):** Enforces strong cryptographic authentication between communicating services, ensuring integrity and confidentiality.

- **Rate Limiting:** Controls the volume of incoming requests to prevent overwhelming services.

- **Access Control Policies:** Define and enforce rules on who can communicate with specific services, minimizing exposure.

- **Endpoint Hardening:** Regularly updating and patching services to guard against exploits.

```
apiVersion: networking.k8s.io/v1
kind: NetworkPolicy
metadata:
  name: restrict-access
  namespace: production
spec:
  podSelector:
    matchLabels:
      app: payments
  ingress:
  - from:
    - podSelector:
        matchLabels:
          access: internal
  policyTypes:
  - Ingress
```

In this example, access to the payments service is restricted to internal pods labeled appropriately, mitigating unauthorized access attempts.

Employing a defense-in-depth strategy ensures multiple layers of security, so if one control fails, others stand to protect. This approach encompasses multiple security controls across different layers:

## 5.6. HANDLING EXTERNAL THREATS

- **Network Layer Protections:** Leverage network policies and firewalls to restrict access, filter traffic, and enforce segmentation.
- **Service Layer Security:** Implement mTLS, authenticate services, and regularly review endpoints to harden service interfaces.
- **Application Layer Controls:** Incorporate web application firewalls (WAFs), sanitize inputs, and monitor for anomalous application behaviors.
- **Traffic Monitoring:** Use telemetry data to continuously monitor and analyze traffic, identifying patterns that suggest an active threat.

A defense-in-depth approach enhances resilience by integrating these layers, ensuring robust protection against a spectrum of external threats.

DDoS attacks pose significant risk by disrupting availability, thus negatively impacting services. Linkerd and the underlying Kubernetes ecosystem provide mechanisms to mitigate such attacks:

- **Rate Limiting:** Prevents abuse by restricting the number of requests a service can handle in a given timeframe, configured via Linkerd annotations or custom controllers.

```
apiVersion: config.linkerd.io/v1
kind: RateLimit
metadata:
  name: payments-rate-limit
  namespace: production
spec:
  maxRequestsPerSecond: 100
  burst: 50
  rules:
  - selector: "app=payments"
```

- **Autoscaling:** Automatically adjusts service instances based on demand, providing adaptability to tolerate high loads.
- **Traffic Scrubbing:** Redirects traffic through scrubbing centers that filter out malicious traffic and pass only legitimate requests.

Linkerd supports comprehensive monitoring and incident response frameworks, crucial in detecting and responding to security threats effectively. Tools like Prometheus and Grafana offer detailed insights into microservice health and behavior:

- **Anomaly Detection:** Set up alerts on unusual traffic patterns, response times, or error rates that may signify an ongoing attack.
- **Real-Time Alerting:** Notify security teams immediately upon detecting suspicious activities, allowing prompt action to mitigate threats.
- **Rapid Incident Response:** Implement escalation procedures, designate response teams, and rehearse response plans for timely containment of threats.

Implementing monitoring example:

```
alerting:
  alertmanagers:
  - static_configs:
    - targets: ['alertmanager:9093']
groups:
- name: high-traffic.rules
  rules:
  - alert: HighRequestRate
    expr: rate(http_requests_total[1m]) > 100
    for: 5m
    labels:
      severity: critical
    annotations:
      summary: "High Request Rate Detected"
      description: "The request rate for {{ $labels.service }} has exceeded 100 requests
          per second."
```

Adopting a zero trust security model strengthens the defenses against external threats. This model operates under the assumption that all users and traffic are potential threats, thereby requiring stringent verification and minimal trust.

Core principles of a zero trust model include:

- **Strict Identity Verification:** Continuously authenticate and authorize every access request within the network.
- **Micro-Segmentation:** Partition networks into smaller segments within which access is tightly controlled and monitored.

- **Least Privilege Access:** Only grant permissions absolutely necessary for the function, curtailing potential damage from compromised credentials.

These measures resoundingly reinforce security postures, ensuring that external threats face impediments at every access attempt.

Even with stringent protections, it's imperative to have robust incident response and forensic capabilities to minimize damage in the event of a breach:

- **Incident Logging:** Keep detailed logs of all incidents and the responses enacted, providing a basis for future risk assessments.

- **Post-Incident Review:** Conduct thorough reviews after incidents to identify lessons learned and improve resilience.

- **Forensic Analysis:** Investigate breaches with a forensic approach to trace the origin, evaluate the impact, and learn about exploitable points.

Regular audits and penetration tests are critical in identifying unseen vulnerabilities and validating security controls against expert-led attack simulations:

- **Security Audits:** Systematic evaluations of infrastructure, configuration, and policies help identify and mitigate vulnerabilities.

- **Penetration Testing:** Engage cybersecurity professionals to simulate attacks and expose weaknesses, facilitating measured improvements.

- **Continuous Improvement:** Regularly update security measures and practices based on audit and testing insights, adapting to evolving threat landscapes.

Handling external threats in Linkerd involves a multi-faceted approach incorporating layered defense, vigilant monitoring, and proactive response measures. By fortifying microservices through rigorous security controls and adopting a zero trust model, organizations significantly bolster their defenses against potential threats, ensuring the security and availability of services in an increasingly hostile digital landscape.

# Chapter 6

# Traffic Management in Linkerd

Traffic management in Linkerd is pivotal for optimizing the flow of requests across microservices. This chapter focuses on the mechanisms that facilitate sophisticated traffic control, including techniques like traffic splitting and canary releases for progressive delivery of services. It examines request routing policies and how service discovery is integrated to streamline communication pathways. Additionally, the chapter discusses Linkerd's load balancing algorithms and the implementation of circuit breakers to maintain system stability and resilience. Together, these functions allow for precise control over traffic patterns, enhancing both the performance and reliability of service interactions.

## 6.1 Traffic Splitting and Canary Releases

Traffic splitting and canary releases are fundamental strategies in the domain of progressive delivery, enabling developers to test new service versions in a production environment with minimal risk. In Linkerd, these practices are supported natively to facilitate safe and controlled deployments. This section delves into the mechanisms by which Linkerd achieves these goals, examining the technical aspects of traffic splitting and canary releases in detail.

Traffic splitting involves distributing incoming requests among different versions of a service. This distribution can be based on a variety of criteria, such as percentage-based splits or specific user segments. By routing a small portion of traffic to a new service version, teams can observe system behavior and user response, minimizing the potential impact of defects.

A canary release is a technique where a new service version is gradually introduced to a subset of users before being rolled out to the entire user base. The term "canary" is derived from the historical use of canaries in coal mines to detect toxic gases; similarly, canary releases help detect issues with new software changes before they affect the entire system. In Linkerd, implementing canary releases involves several key steps, each critical to ensuring the desired governance over service behavior and user experience.

Linkerd allows for sophisticated traffic splitting capabilities through TrafficSplit resources, which are part of the Service Mesh Interface (SMI) specifications. A TrafficSplit is a custom resource definition (CRD) that defines how traffic intended for a specific service should be divided among different service backends. The following YAML configuration illustrates a basic TrafficSplit setup that distributes traffic between two service versions:

```
apiVersion: split.smi-spec.io/v1alpha1
kind: TrafficSplit
metadata:
  name: example-split
  namespace: default
spec:
  service: my-service
  backends:
  - service: my-service-v1
    weight: 90
  - service: my-service-v2
    weight: 10
```

In this configuration, my-service receives requests that are divided between my-service-v1 and my-service-v2 in a 90-10 weight ratio. Linkerd ensures that 90% of the traffic is routed to my-service-v1, the stable ver-

## 6.1. TRAFFIC SPLITTING AND CANARY RELEASES

sion, while 10% is directed to my-service-v2, the canary version. The flexibility provided by the TrafficSplit specification allows developers to adjust weights dynamically and roll out releases gradually, adjusting overall exposure as confidence in the new version grows.

The implementation of canary releases in Linkerd involves monitoring and observability tools to assess the performance of the canary version. Metrics such as success rates, error rates, latency, and user-generated feedback are crucial in determining whether to proceed with a full rollout or rollback the changes. Linkerd's integration with Prometheus offers a comprehensive mechanism for collecting and analyzing these metrics. Below is a sample Prometheus query targeting HTTP request success rates:

sum(rate(http_request_total{service="my-service-v2"}[5m])) / sum(rate(http_request_total{service="my-service"}[5m])) < 0.99

This query calculates the success rate of requests on the my-service-v2 canary version over a five-minute window. If the success rate falls below 99%, developers may decide to halt additional traffic or initiate a rollback.

A rollback, the process of reverting traffic to the stable version, can also be managed through Linkerd's TrafficSplit resources by updating service weights. The combination of observability insights and SMI resource controls empowers developers to manage risks proactively and ensure high availability and reliability across the service mesh.

To further enhance the robustness of traffic splitting, Linkerd supports advanced techniques such as A/B testing and blue-green deployments. These methodologies build upon traffic splitting's fundamental principles, allowing for deeper experimentation and more nuanced traffic control. A/B testing allows developers to evaluate different service versions against predefined metrics, optimizing user experience through data-driven insights.

Below is a sample configuration illustrating a scenario with A/B testing. Here, user traffic is split between two distinct features being evaluated:

```
apiVersion: split.smi-spec.io/v1alpha1
kind: TrafficSplit
metadata:
  name: ab-test-feature
```

```
  namespace: default
spec:
  service: service-ab-test
  backends:
  - service: feature-a
    weight: 50
  - service: feature-b
    weight: 50
```

In this A/B testing scenario, the traffic is split equally between feature-a and feature-b. As with canary releases, continuous monitoring and data analysis are vital for evaluating the impact and success of each experimental feature.

When deploying canary releases and executing traffic splitting strategies, automation tools such as Helm or ArgoCD can facilitate repeatable, scalable, and near-zero-downtime deployments. For example, a Helm chart can be constructed to encapsulate the TrafficSplit definition alongside other deployment configurations, enabling version-controlled, template-driven rollout processes.

Finally, compliance and security considerations are cornerstones of any robust traffic splitting and canary release strategy. This includes crafting policies for compliance with industry regulations, as well as mechanisms for ensuring secure and authorized access to service resources. Linkerd's mutual TLS (mTLS) capability provides end-to-end encryption, ensuring secure service-to-service communication and protecting data integrity as traffic is rerouted among versions.

The following is an example of how to programmatically manage mTLS for services engaged in traffic splitting with Linkerd:

```
apiVersion: linkerd.io/v1alpha1
kind: ServiceProfile
metadata:
  name: my-service.linkerd
  namespace: default
spec:
  routes:
  - name: /my-service-endpoint
    condition:
      method: GET
    retryBudget:
      ttl: 10s
      retryRatio: 0.2
      minRetriesPerSecond: 10
```

In combination with ServiceProfiles, Linkerd's mTLS functionality enables secure and reliable interactions, ensuring that all service communication adheres to defined security policies throughout the traffic splitting and canary release processes.

This comprehensive approach to testing and deploying new service versions positions teams to effectively manage production risks and innovate with confidence. Linkerd's native capabilities for traffic splitting and canary releases provide a structured, reliable framework that integrates seamlessly with existing ecosystem tools, extending progressive delivery practices within modern microservices architectures.

## 6.2 Request Routing and Service Discovery

Effectively managing request routing and service discovery in a microservices architecture is crucial for optimizing service interactions and achieving high performance. Within the Linkerd service mesh, these functionalities are automated to maximize network efficiency and support seamless communication pathways between services. This section explores the underlying principles and implementation details of request routing and service discovery as executed by Linkerd.

Request routing in Linkerd orchestrates the pathway that requests take from client to service, leveraging intelligent routing decisions based on the current state of the network, service health, and policy definitions. At its core, Linkerd employs a sidecar proxy architecture, where each service instance is accompanied by a Linkerd proxy that intercepts and manages its network traffic. This proxy layer abstracts the complexity of routing decisions, facilitating consistent and efficient request handling across the service mesh.

Linkerd uses a dedicated control plane to manage configuration and network topology, disseminating pertinent information to proxies. This decouples routing logic from application code, allowing developers to focus on business logic rather than networking concerns. To better illustrate this, the following service topology diagram demonstrates the relationship between services, proxies, and the Linkerd control plane.

## CHAPTER 6. TRAFFIC MANAGEMENT IN LINKERD

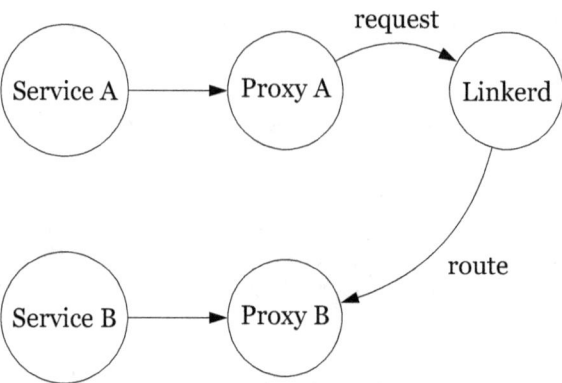

Service discovery in Linkerd complements request routing by dynamically discovering service instances and updating the routing table accordingly. Linkerd seamlessly integrates with service registries—such as Kubernetes service discovery—to obtain the current location and availability status of services within the mesh. This dynamic capability ensures zero downtime and resiliency in service communications, even amidst scaling events or failures.

A fundamental component of Linkerd's routing mechanism is the 'ServiceProfile', a custom resource used to define routing policies and service-level objectives. The ServiceProfile CRD allows developers to specify expected service behaviors, rate limits, retry logic, and timeouts to ensure services adhere to operational expectations. Below is an example of a ServiceProfile for a hypothetical service, 'my-service'.

```
apiVersion: linkerd.io/v1alpha1
kind: ServiceProfile
metadata:
  name: my-service.default.svc.cluster.local
  namespace: default
spec:
  routes:
  - name: '/get-data'
    condition:
      method: GET
    isRetryable: true
    timeout: 1s
    retryBudget:
      minRetriesPerSecond: 10
      retryRatio: 0.2
      ttl: 10s
```

## 6.2. REQUEST ROUTING AND SERVICE DISCOVERY

This ServiceProfile specifies that requests matching the 'GET' method for the '/get-data' route are retryable, with a timeout threshold and specified retry budget. This configuration empowers the Linkerd data plane to maintain service quality by retrying failed requests within controlled limits, preventing systemic overloads.

For advanced routing and service discovery, Linkerd supports integration with Distributed Tracing tools, such as OpenTelemetry or Jaeger. These integrations allow for enhanced observability into service request paths, bottlenecks, and latency issues. A distributed trace can be visualized to diagnose the time taken by each service along a request's journey, highlighting inefficiencies in routing or service discovery.

A simplified distributed trace can be imagined with this serialized execution path: client request, proxy interception, service resolution, upstream request, and downstream response. Monitoring tools can capture and present this sequence to illuminate the interactions across services:

[Client Request]->[Resolved by Proxy]->[Service A]->[Service B]->[Service C]->[Response]

Security is a critical concern in request routing and service discovery, especially in diverse and complex microservice environments. Linkerd employs mutual TLS (mTLS) to provide end-to-end encryption of service-to-service communication, ensuring both secure data transmission and trusted identity verification. This secure channel is established automatically by Linkerd's data plane proxies, providing peace of mind for sensitive communications.

To ensure configuration simplicity and maintainability, Linkerd abstracts much of the complexity inherent in manual service discovery and routing management. By leveraging service meshes like Linkerd, organizations benefit from a reduction in service discovery configuration overhead, fostering greater agility and deployment flexibility.

The following configuration file demonstrates how to enable mTLS across all services in a Kubernetes cluster managed by Linkerd:

```
apiVersion: v1
kind: Namespace
metadata:
  name: default
  annotations:
```

```
    linkerd.io/inject: enabled

---
apiVersion: linkerd.io/v1alpha1
kind: Identity
metadata:
  name: trust-anchor
spec:
  trustAnchorsPem: |
    -----BEGIN CERTIFICATE-----
    MIIBIjANBgkqh...
    -----END CERTIFICATE-----
```

With mTLS enabled, communication between services remains encrypted with cryptographic assurance, thus fulfilling data security and integrity requirements in regulated environments and underscoring best practices in microservice security.

The integration of request routing with Linkerd's service discovery capabilities forms the backbone of link-layer networking in modern cloud-native applications. This sophisticated architecture ensures agility, reliability, and efficiency in service interactions, underpinning successful operations and digital transformations in cloud-native environments.

Linkerd's holistic approach to request routing and service discovery provides a robust foundation for developing scalable, secure, and resilient microservice architectures. By automating these critical network operations within the service mesh, Linkerd enables developers to deploy applications with confidence, ensuring optimized traffic flows and service availability across complex environments.

## 6.3 Load Balancing Algorithms

Load balancing is a critical component in distributed systems, designed to optimize resource utilization, maximize throughput, minimize response time, and avoid overload on any single resource. Within the domain of microservices and service meshes, Linkerd provides advanced load balancing algorithms to distribute traffic effectively across multiple service instances. This section examines the various load balancing strategies employed by Linkerd, their implementations, and the criteria by which they are selected.

## 6.3. LOAD BALANCING ALGORITHMS

Linkerd's load balancing capabilities are implemented through its data plane proxy, which handles service requests and decides which service instance the request should be routed to. The choice of load balancing algorithm can significantly affect the performance and reliability of applications, especially at scale.

- **Round Robin Load Balancing:** Round Robin is one of the simplest and most widely implemented load balancing algorithms. It involves distributing requests sequentially across the service instances in a cyclical order. Each service instance gets a request in turn, which ensures equal distribution over time.

  The Round Robin algorithm is highly effective in scenarios where there are uniform instances and a consistent flow of requests. However, its simplicity can become a limitation if service instances have varying capabilities or the number of requests fluctuates significantly.

  ```
  # List of service instances
  instances = [Instance1, Instance2, Instance3, Instance4]
  index = 0

  def round_robin():
      global index
      instance = instances[index]
      index = (index + 1) % len(instances)
      return instance
  ```

  In the above pseudocode, requests are distributed across a static list of instances. The modulo operation ensures that the index wraps around to the start of the list after reaching the end.

- **Least Connections Load Balancing:** The Least Connections algorithm directs traffic to the service instance with the least number of active connections. It is particularly advantageous in environments where requests can have varying durations. By continuously monitoring the load on each instance, this algorithm ensures that no single instance is disproportionately burdened.

  Linkerd monitors real-time metrics on connection counts through its proxies, dynamically directing requests to minimize delays. The algorithm is computationally straightforward yet adapts effectively to varying traffic patterns.

```
# Dictionary mapping instance to active connections
active_connections = {Instance1: 3, Instance2: 2, Instance3: 1}

def least_connections():
    return min(active_connections, key=active_connections.get)
```

In this example, the 'min' function returns the instance with the fewest connections, promoting even load distribution based on connection count.

- **Random Load Balancing:** Random load balancing distributes requests probabilistically across available instances. Unlike Round Robin or Least Connections, which rely on deterministic criteria, the Random algorithm can be effective in environments with numerous, equally capable service instances. This approach can avoid the potential for synchronous oscillations that might occur in other deterministic algorithms, offering a simple yet robust mechanism for balancing loads.

  While the Random algorithm does not inherently account for instance load or response times, its simplicity and low overhead make it suitable for certain high-throughput scenarios.

```
import random

def random_choice():
    return random.choice(instances)
```

- **Weighted Least Request Load Balancing:** Weighted Least Request combines the principles of both Least Connections and weight-based algorithms. Each service instance can be assigned a weight that reflects its capacity or priority level, adjusting for computing power, memory, or deployment constraints. The algorithm routes fewer requests to instances with lower weights, effectively balancing traffic in proportion to capacity.

  In Linkerd, weights can be dynamically configured based on metrics such as CPU load or memory usage, providing a flexible framework for managing heterogeneous clusters.

```
# Dictionary mapping instances to [connections, weight]
instance_data = {Instance1: [4, 2], Instance2: [2, 4], Instance3: [1, 1]}

def weighted_least_request():
    weighted_instances = [
        (connections/weight, instance)
```

## 6.3. LOAD BALANCING ALGORITHMS

```
        for instance, (connections, weight) in instance_data.items()
]
return min(weighted_instances)[1]
```

This technique enables an adaptive, context-aware decision-making process, guiding requests optimally within the resource constraints available.

- **Power of Two Choices Load Balancing:** The Power of Two Choices is an efficient algorithmic strategy that maintains simplicity while providing a high level of randomness to prevent clustering. This algorithm randomly picks two instances and then chooses the instance with fewer connections. This dual-sampling approach significantly reduces the probability of imbalance.

```
import random

def power_of_two_choices():
    choice1 = random.choice(instances)
    choice2 = random.choice(instances)
    return min(
        [choice1, choice2],
        key=lambda instance: active_connections[instance]
    )
```

This approach achieves near-optimal performance using minimal state information, making it valuable in managing large-scale systems without the complexity of centralized coordination.

- **Service Mesh Integration:** In Linkerd, load balancing algorithms are enhanced by the mesh's comprehensive visibility and metric collection capabilities. The service mesh architecture inherently supports monitoring, which gathers data on request rates, success rates, latencies, and utilization factors. This data-driven oversight enables the selection of the most suitable load balancing algorithm based on real-time network dynamics.

Linkerd's utilization of Destination and Identity services facilitates the sharing of service state information, allowing proxies to make informed routing decisions dynamically. By pairing these insights with advanced load balancing techniques, Linkerd delivers a scalable, resilient infrastructure for microservices communication.

```
apiVersion: v1
kind: ConfigMap
```

```
metadata:
  name: linkerd-config
data:
  global: |
    proxy:
      loadBalancer:
        mode: least_conn
```

- **Adaptive Load Balancing in Hybrid Clouds:** In hybrid cloud settings, spanning on-premises and cloud environments, adaptive load balancing becomes crucial. Linkerd can optimize load distribution across heterogeneous platforms by evaluating latency differences, instance types, and geographical constraints. This adaptability reduces latency and resource costs, aligning traffic patterns with business priorities.

  By leveraging Linkerd's robust telemetry and observability features, operators can map service dependencies, ensuring alignment with SLAs regardless of deployment environments. The alignment of traffic loads with system capacities enhances both resilience and performance, crucial for operational efficiency in hybrid setups.

Comprehensively, Linkerd's suite of load balancing algorithms fosters an architecture optimal for cloud-native environments, where agility and responsiveness dictate success. By selecting appropriate algorithms based on dynamic load characteristics and infrastructure, Linkerd empowers service reliability, user experience, and cost-effectiveness across expanding microservices ecosystems.

## 6.4 Circuit Breaking for Resilience

In microservice architectures, resilience is a core attribute that ensures system stability and reliability under variable operational conditions. Circuit breaking is an essential pattern leveraged to enhance resilience, preventing request overloads and isolating failing components to protect system integrity. Within Linkerd, circuit breaking mechanisms are seamlessly integrated to provide robust defenses against cascading failures that can result from distressed service dependencies.

## 6.4. CIRCUIT BREAKING FOR RESILIENCE

Circuit breakers function analogously to electrical circuit breakers; they detect faults and disable paths to prevent failures from propagating. In a computing context, a circuit breaker can interrupt an operation if it detects a pattern of failure, thereby allowing the underlying service time to recover. This contrasts with retry mechanisms, which might perpetuate further load on already struggling services.

A circuit breaker is typically defined with three states: Closed, Open, and Half-Open.

- **Closed State:** In its default state, requests flow unimpeded. The breaker monitors for failures.

- **Open State:** Upon detecting failures exceeding a defined threshold, the circuit opens, stopping further requests from passing through. Instead, errors are returned to calling clients instantly.

- **Half-Open State:** After a defined timeout, the circuit transitions to this tentative state, permitting a limited number of test requests to gauge if the service has recovered. Depending on their success, the circuit may return to a closed or open state.

Linkerd utilizes a combination of weighted routing policies and response metrics to determine circuit breaker states. Linkerd's default telemetry gathering facilitates the real-time collection of service health metrics, forming the basis for circuit breaking decisions.

```
apiVersion: linkerd.io/v1alpha1
kind: ServiceProfile
metadata:
  name: failure-prone-service.default.svc.cluster.local
spec:
  routes:
    - name: "/api/request"
      circuitBreaker:
        successThreshold: 20
        maxFailures: 5
        resetTimeout: 60s
```

In this configuration, a circuit breaker is applied to the '/api/request' route of 'failure-prone-service'. It transitions to an open state after five consecutive failed requests, retrying the circuit after 60 seconds, requiring 20 successful requests to reclose.

During normal operation, service requests pass unhindered. However, if a surge in requests accompanies failing services, the circuit breaker activates to prevent excessive timeout or error handling on client-side applications. This control mechanism ensures that resources are conserved, protecting vital system components from being swamped by repeated failure-induced calls.

Under varying traffic conditions, circuit breaker parameters such as 'maxFailures' and 'resetTimeout' should be adjustable to reflect service capacity and acceptable risk levels. For example, low-latency critical paths could tolerate tighter thresholds for faster recovery to sustained reliability.

Circuit breaking works synergistically with retry and timeout policies to enhance resilience:

- **Retries:** Allow attempts to be made on slightly failing requests. Upon exceeding retries, the circuit breaker avoids further well-intentioned retries from overloading the resource.
- **Timeouts:** Ensure failure detection is speedy, triggering the circuit to open more decisively. The combination assures prompt response adjustments when anomalies arise.

Empirical testing in production environments should calibrate retry and timeout periods parallel to circuit breaker sensitivity to optimally align with performance objectives.

Trace tools within Linkerd's observability suite, incorporating Jaeger, provide clarity into circuit breaker behavior. A sequence graph may be utilized to visualize request paths, showing at what point circuit-breaking occurs.

```
[Normal Requests] -> [Anomalies Detected] -> [Circuit Opens]
                              |
              [Circuit Half-Opens] <- [Reset Timeout]
                              |
              [Circuit Re-Closes on Success]
```

This visualizer offers an intuitive portrayal of service resilience, aiding diagnostics and future tuning efforts.

Linkerd facilitates the deployment of advanced strategies like Rate-Limited and Service Degradation:

- **Rate-Limited Circuits:** Restrict the rate of allowed requests during a half-open state, enabling service recovery while assessing the reliability of the service.

- **Degradation Protocols:** Progressive reductions in service provided (fallback operations) in circuit open states maintain service assurances under lower expectations.

These strategies help achieve nuanced control over critical requests, maintaining essential service functionality during periods of duress.

Load metrics and error rates directly feed back into circuit breaker configurations, refining responsiveness and ensuring reactionary improvements are incremental rather than disruptive. CI/CD pipelines may leverage synthetic tests to validate circuit breaker responses, exposing edge cases proactively.

By embedding circuit breaking within the service mesh framework, Linkerd empowers developers with an essential resilience toolkit. Through the intelligent monitoring and fast failover of compromised components, healthy service interactions and overall system stability are preserved. Circuit breakers act as a safeguard, overseeing delicate balances between reliability and service performance without extensive manual intervention.

In operationalizing circuit breaking strategies, organizations refine their ability to maintain SLAs and achieve predictable recovery in modern, dynamic microservice ecosystems. As applications scale and become increasingly distributed, Linkerd's circuit-breaking capabilities become indispensable, safeguarding both the continuity and quality of service delivery.

## 6.5 Managing Latency and Timeouts

Latency and timeouts are critical aspects of microservice performance management, with direct implications on user experiences and system reliability. Effective management of these parameters is essential to ensure timely responses and maintain the equilibrium of inter-service communications. Linkerd, as a service mesh, provides comprehensive tools and mechanisms for observing, controlling, and optimizing these factors across distributed systems. This section explores strategies for managing latency and configuring timeouts effectively within Linkerd deployments.

Latency refers to the delay incurred when one service communicates with another across the network. This delay can result from various factors, including network transmission times, processing delays within service instances, and data serialization/deserialization overheads. In microservices architectures, where multiple services orchestrate to fulfill user requests, minimizing latency is vital to prevent the cumulative buildup that can degrade performance.

Network latency can be influenced by geographical distances, network paths, and bandwidth limitations. Computational latency, conversely, stems from application logic complexity and resource constraints. Both require targeted approaches to manage effectively.

Timeouts are designed to prevent indefinite waiting times for operations that may be delayed or failed. By enforcing a maximum wait duration, timeouts help identify malfunctioning components and trigger appropriate fallback or retry mechanisms. In Linkerd, configuring timeouts strategically allows services to degrade gracefully without affecting system-wide operations considerably.

The balancing act between latency and timeout settings ensures that user requests are met promptly without prematurely abandoning operations that might be successful.

Linkerd enables developers to define latency and timeout policies using Service Profiles. By specifying these properties in YAML configurations, Linkerd orchestrates request handling through the data plane proxies, automatically enforcing timeout settings and observing latency characteristics for each service route.

```
apiVersion: linkerd.io/v1alpha1
kind: ServiceProfile
metadata:
  name: hyper-service.default.svc.cluster.local
spec:
  routes:
    - name: "/fetch-data"
      condition:
        method: GET
      timeout: 500ms
    - name: "/submit-order"
```

## 6.5. MANAGING LATENCY AND TIMEOUTS

```
condition:
    method: POST
timeout: 1s
```

In this example, the '/fetch-data' and '/submit-order' routes of 'hyper-service' have different timeout settings, reflecting their service-level expectations and operational characteristics. Adjustments to these policies must consider typical response times and acceptable delay durations for critical processes.

Effective latency management requires ongoing visibility into request-response patterns throughout the service mesh. Linkerd seamlessly integrates with Prometheus and OpenTelemetry to provide deep insights into latency metrics and distributed tracing. These tools empower operators with detailed data on request timing, including commercial tools like Grafana that can create visual dashboards showing latency trends.

A sample Prometheus query to monitor average request latency would look as follows:

```
rate(request_duration_seconds_sum{job="linkerd-proxy"}[5m]) /
rate(request_duration_seconds_count{job="linkerd-proxy"}[5m])
```

This query calculates the average duration of requests handled by Linkerd proxies over a five-minute interval. Anomalies in observed trends can indicate emerging performance issues, triggering intervention before service degradation affects user experiences significantly.

To reduce network-induced latency:

- Implement caching to store frequently accessed data, reducing redundant fetch operations.
- Use Content Delivery Networks (CDN) to distribute assets geographically closer to user locations.
- Optimize API design and payload sizes to decrease data transmission times.

Minimizing computationally-induced latency:

- Employ micro-optimizations in code for hotspots and critical path operations.

- Utilize asynchronous processing to avoid blocking on slow I/O operations.

- Deploy autoscaling policies to dynamically adjust the compute capacity, addressing peak demand periods swiftly.

By optimizing these parameters collectively, latency reductions have pivotal impacts on the overall responsiveness of applications.

Timeout configurations should be tailored specifically to the nature and importance of each service call:

- Shorten timeouts for idempotent read requests or background task invocations, minimizing wasted time on slower service instances.

- Lengthen timeouts for essential transactions or order submissions, allowing greater flexibility in user interactions and backend processing.

- Implement exponential back-off strategies for retries, balancing immediate failure responses with optimism towards transient issue resolution.

User perception of performance is instrumental in defining the success of web applications, with even minor delays affecting abandonment rates or transaction completions. Timeouts that frequently lead to dropped requests can exacerbate user dissatisfaction, leading to churn. Thus, concerted optimizations in latency responses strengthen competitive positions and foster retention.

Through A/B testing and user feedback loops, developers can fine-tune latency and timeout configurations, implementing empirically-validated settings that enhance satisfaction and adherence to Service-Level Agreements (SLAs).

The adept management of latency and timeout settings within a service mesh context is essential for creating performant, reliable applications. By utilizing Linkerd's service profiles, telemetry integrations, and dynamic configuration capabilities, organizations can systematically address these facets, streamlining seamless and satisfactory user interactions.

The capabilities Linkerd provides offer developers substantial opportunities to optimize service communications, adapt to real-world challenges, and build resilience against changing demands or network conditions. Through vigilant monitoring and iterative refinement, latency and timeout management become keystones of operational excellence in modern microservices deployments.

## 6.6 Advanced Traffic Policies

Advanced traffic policies are critical for managing and optimizing the flow of network traffic across complex microservice architectures. Within service mesh frameworks like Linkerd, these policies enable sophisticated control over request routing, security, access control, and quality of service (QoS) metrics. Implementing advanced policies ensures applications remain performant, secure, and resilient while meeting diverse operational requirements and business goals. This section explores the design, implementation, and management of advanced traffic policies within Linkerd.

Traffic segmentation involves dividing traffic into distinct classes based on various criteria such as source, identity, destination, or content type. Priority routing then utilizes this segmentation to prioritize handling for different traffic classes, ensuring that critical requests receive preferential treatment.

For instance, requests originating from VIP users or service accounts needing expedited handling can be prioritized. Linkerd leverages identity-based policies to implement these concepts, tying service profiles to Kubernetes identity mechanisms or external identity providers (like OAuth) for fine-grained access control.

```
apiVersion: linkerd.io/v1alpha1
kind: ServiceProfile
metadata:
  name: important-service.default.svc.cluster.local
spec:
  routes:
  - name: "/vip-request"
    condition:
      headers:
        user-tier: vip
    isTimeout: 200ms
    priority: high
```

```
- name: "/standard-request"
  condition:
    headers:
      user-tier: standard
  isTimeout: 500ms
```

In the above example, requests bearing a 'vip' user-tier header are assigned higher priority, meaning they may see reduced latencies and tighter timeout settings compared to standard requests.

Rate limiting is a crucial policy in managing traffic loads, preventing abuse, and ensuring fair resource allocation among different users or services. Linkerd, through Service Profiles, supports implementing rate limitation policies to control the rate of incoming requests.

Rate limiting can be implemented globally, per user, per service, or even per endpoint. Techniques such as token bucket algorithms or leaky bucket algorithms are typically employed to manage and enforce these policies.

```
apiVersion: linkerd.io/v1alpha1
kind: ServiceProfile
metadata:
  name: throttled-service.default.svc.cluster.local
spec:
  routes:
    - name: "/api-endpoint"
      condition:
        method: GET
      rateLimit:
        maxRequestsPerSecond: 100
```

Here, the 'throttled-service' is configured to support up to 100 requests per second for the '/api-endpoint', leveraging an in-line specification within the service profile. This effectively prevents overwhelming the service, ensuring sustainable operations.

Traffic mirroring is a technique that involves duplicating live traffic from production services and sending it to another service instance for testing purposes. This approach allows real-world data to be utilized in validating the new instances without interfering with live operations.

In Linkerd, traffic mirroring can be orchestrated via configuration directives, enabling canary deployments or blue-green deployments. These strategies minimize risks by isolating changes to non-user facing services until thorough validation occurs.

## 6.6. ADVANCED TRAFFIC POLICIES

```
apiVersion: split.smi-spec.io/v1alpha2
kind: TrafficSplit
metadata:
  name: mirror-setup
  namespace: default
spec:
  service: production-service
  backends:
  - service: staging-service
    weight: 0
  mirrors:
  - service: mirror-service
    percent: 10
```

This configuration results in 10% of the incoming traffic being mirrored to 'mirror-service', allowing for seamless testing and validation parallel to live operations as part of a blue-green deployment strategy.

Security policies are indispensable for advanced traffic management in service mesh environments. Linkerd supports mutual TLS (mTLS) for service-to-service communication to ensure encrypted and authenticated messaging. Implementing mTLS ensures data security and protects against man-in-the-middle attacks, a paramount consideration in distributed architectures.

```
apiVersion: linkerd.io/v1alpha1
kind: Identity
metadata:
  name: secure-service.identity.linkerd.cluster.local
spec:
  trustDomain: cluster.local
  identityPEM: |
    -----BEGIN CERTIFICATE-----
    MIIDXT...
    -----END CERTIFICATE-----
  issuers:
  - crtPEM: |
      -----BEGIN CERTIFICATE-----
      MIIDXT...
      -----END CERTIFICATE-----
    keyPEM: |
      -----BEGIN PRIVATE KEY-----
      MIIEvg...
      -----END PRIVATE KEY-----
```

This configuration applies mTLS to the 'secure-service', ensuring all communications conform to strict security standards.

Advanced traffic policies require comprehensive observability and monitoring to confirm they operate effectively. Linkerd, equipped with integrations like Prometheus and Grafana, supports tracking metrics like response times, throughput, error rates, and policy-based metrics like request distributions or rate limits.

Administrators utilize this data to assess policy effectiveness, detecting anomalies or policy breaches instantaneously. Trend analysis assists in tuning policies iteratively, aligning them with evolving business strategies and regulatory requirements.

```
rate(linkerd_tcp_accept_total{namespace='default'}[5m])
```

This Prometheus query monitors TCP acceptance rates within the specified namespace over a five-minute window, providing insights into incoming request patterns.

Advanced traffic policies orchestrated through Linkerd enable the nuanced control demanded by modern microservices architectures. By leveraging granular traffic segmentation, rate limiting, secure communications, and strategic deployment tactics, organizations optimize resource utilization, bolster security, and deliver consistent service performance.

The efficacy of such policies is reinforced by integrating observability into their lifecycle, ensuring adaptability to new challenges and scaling opportunities. Linkerd equips developers with a sophisticated toolkit, paving the way toward refined application delivery and operational excellence.

## Chapter 7

# Monitoring and Observability with Linkerd

Monitoring and observability are critical aspects of maintaining a healthy service mesh, and Linkerd offers robust tools to achieve this. This chapter outlines how Linkerd collects metrics and provides real-time dashboards for visualizing the state of the mesh. It includes discussions on integrating tracing and logging to facilitate detailed analysis of request flows and performance bottlenecks. The chapter also covers alerting systems to promptly inform administrators of anomalies. Emphasizing the use of Prometheus for granular data collection and Grafana for advanced visualization, these tools work together to provide comprehensive insights into service health and performance trends.

## 7.1 Metrics Collection and Dashboarding

Linkerd facilitates robust monitoring and observability through efficient metrics collection and real-time dashboarding capabilities. Central to Linkerd's observability feature is the collection of telemetry data that provides critical insights into service performance, enabling operators to maintain and optimize the health of a service mesh.

Linkerd employs Prometheus as its underlying metrics collection tool. Prometheus is a powerful open-source systems monitoring and alerting toolkit that is widely used for collecting and querying real-time metrics data. In the context of Linkerd, Prometheus collects metrics such as request counts, success rates, and latency distributions from Linkerd's proxies that are part of the data plane.

Several vital metrics are collected by Linkerd, including:

- **Request Count**: This indicates the total number of requests made to a service. By monitoring request counts, operators can identify trends in service usage and detect spikes that may indicate unusual activity or performance bottlenecks.

- **Success Rate**: This metric reflects the percentage of successful responses compared to the total number of requests. A declining success rate can be an early indicator of issues within the service that require investigation.

- **Latency Distribution**: Latency distribution metrics reveal the time taken for requests to traverse the service mesh. They help in identifying slow services or interactions and understanding the overall flow of requests in the mesh.

Metrics collection is initiated by Linkerd's control plane components, which automatically configure Prometheus to scrape metrics from Linkerd proxies. The data collection is performed periodically at specified intervals, ensuring up-to-date information is always available for analysis.

```
scrape_configs:
  - job_name: 'linkerd'
    metrics_path: /metrics
    static_configs:
```

## 7.1. METRICS COLLECTION AND DASHBOARDING

```
    - targets: ['127.0.0.1:9090']
```

This YAML configuration snippet shows a basic example of how Prometheus is configured to scrape metrics from Linkerd. The metrics_path specifies the endpoint where metrics are available, and targets define the addresses of the Linkerd proxies.

Real-time dashboards are essential for visualizing this telemetry data. Linkerd offers built-in dashboard capabilities within its control plane UI, enabling operators to quickly assess service health and performance. The dashboards provide a comprehensive view of key metrics and allow for interactive exploration of data:

- **Traffic**: Displays metrics related to requests, including rates, errors, and durations, segmented by service and route. This allows for quick identification of traffic patterns and potential bottlenecks.

- **Latency**: Visual representations of latency distributions help in diagnosing performance issues. Operators can examine percentile distributions to understand outliers and anomalies.

- **Success Rate**: Graphs showing success rates over time are pivotal for ensuring service reliability. Anomalies in success rates can prompt further investigation.

Linkerd's dashboards are powered by Prometheus Query Language (PromQL), which is a flexible query language used to extract information from Prometheus. A fundamental understanding of PromQL can enable users to customize the data shown on dashboards, tailoring visualization to meet specific organizational needs.

```
sum(rate(http_requests_total{status=~"2.."}[1m])) by (service)
  / sum(rate(http_requests_total[1m])) by (service)
```

The above PromQL query calculates the success rate of requests for a specific service by dividing the total number of successful requests (HTTP 2xx responses) by the total number of requests over a one-minute window. This query highlights how metrics can be aggregated and analyzed to derive meaningful insights about service performance.

Beyond built-in dashboards, Linkerd data can also be visualized using external tools like Grafana, which offers advanced features for plot customization and dashboard sharing. Grafana's integration with Prometheus and its extensive visualization capabilities make it an excellent choice for teams that require in-depth analysis and collaboration features.

Linkerd's metrics collection and dashboarding provide a robust framework for observability in the service mesh. By enabling comprehensive monitoring and interactive visualizations, operators can ensure services are optimized for performance and reliability, meeting critical cloud-native application demands. Dashboarding capabilities simplify the identification of issues, performance tuning, and aid in capacity planning, thereby significantly enhancing operational efficiency and ensuring smooth service operation.

## 7.2 Tracing and Logging

In the domain of distributed systems, tracing and logging are fundamental components for monitoring and diagnosing system behavior. Linkerd integrates comprehensive tracing and logging mechanisms to enable operators to track requests effectively and diagnose issues within a service mesh.

Tracing involves tracking the path of a request as it propagates through various services, providing a detailed view of service interactions and latencies associated with each step of the request's journey. Linkerd supports distributed tracing through integration with tools such as Jaeger and Zipkin.

To enable tracing, Linkerd propagates trace context information via HTTP headers. These headers facilitate the correlation of traces across different service boundaries, ensuring a cohesive and end-to-end request visualization. The commonly used headers include:

- x-request-id: A unique identifier for each request, allowing it to be traced across services.

- x-b3-traceid: A unique identifier for a particular trace, used by Zipkin and Jaeger.

## 7.2. TRACING AND LOGGING

- x-b3-spanid: Represents an individual operation within a trace.

- x-b3-parentspanid: Identifies the parent span that the current operation is part of.

These headers are automatically managed by the Linkerd data plane proxies, making it seamless to integrate tracing into existing service architectures.

Linkerd's integration with tracing systems provides detailed visibility into the request flow. Operators can visualize request lifecycles, identify bottlenecks, and analyze service latencies. A typical trace provides:

- **Service-Level Latency**: The time taken for a request to be processed by individual services, highlighting areas where optimizations may be necessary.

- **Inter-Service Communication**: Insights into the network path and dependencies between services in the mesh.

- **Propagation Delays**: Time taken for requests to move between nodes, helping in identifying network issues.

```
{
  "traceId": "a1b2c3d4e5f6g7h8",
  "spans": [
    {
      "id": "abcd1234",
      "parentId": null,
      "name": "get /api/v1/resource",
      "startTime": 1637329200000,
      "duration": 200,
      "serviceName": "frontend",
      "annotations": [...]
    },
    {
      "id": "efgh5678",
      "parentId": "abcd1234",
      "name": "query database",
      "startTime": 1637329200200,
      "duration": 150,
      "serviceName": "backend",
      "annotations": [...]
    }
  ]
}
```

This JSON representation outlines a trace with two spans: a frontend request and a backend database query. Each span documents start times and durations, providing tangible data for performance tuning and analysis.

Logging, on the other hand, provides a complementary approach to tracing by recording discrete events or messages generated during the operation of services. Linkerd employs structured logging to output detailed logs that can be processed programmatically.

Logs are essential for debugging and post-incident analysis, offering granular insight into the behavior of a system at runtime. Key aspects unified by Linkerd's logging capabilities include:

- **Error Logging**: Captures anomalies or exceptions that occur within a service, pivotal for root cause analysis.

- **Access Logs**: Document request and response metadata, including status codes and response times, helpful for auditing and compliance.

- **Event Logs**: Record noteworthy events, such as service start-ups, shutdowns, or configuration changes.

Linkerd logs are structured in JSON or similar formats, conducive to ingestion by log aggregation services like ELK Stack (Elasticsearch, Logstash, Kibana) or Fluentd. This facilitates centralized logging, real-time query execution, and visual analytics.

For example, an application-level error might be logged as follows:

```
{
  "timestamp": "2023-04-01T12:45:00Z",
  "level": "ERROR",
  "service": "payment-gateway",
  "message": "Transaction processing failed",
  "exception": {
    "type": "IOException",
    "message": "Connection reset by peer",
    "stackTrace": [...]
  },
  "correlationId": "d3c4b1a2-3f4e-5b6c-7d8e-9f0a1b2c3d4e"
}
```

Here, the log captures critical information such as the error level, affected service, a descriptive message, exception details, and a correlation ID linked to related requests.

Both tracing and logging are vital for observability in complex microservices environments. Linkerd's integration with these systems helps manage distributed applications more intuitively and reduce the mean time to resolution (MTTR) during service disruptions.

Additionally, Linkerd's logging and tracing capabilities can be configured and customized based on specific operational needs. Configuration of log verbosity, trace sampling rates, and integration endpoints can be tuned to balance between information richness and system performance overhead.

Implementing tracing and logging in Linkerd demands thoughtful planning. Efficient use of these tools involves careful structuring of logs, setting meaningful tracing spans, and leveraging advanced filtering mechanisms to focus on relevant data. By harnessing the full potential of tracing and logging, operators gain a deeper understanding of system dynamics, leading to enhanced reliability and improved user satisfaction.

## 7.3 Alerting and Notifications

In systems and network monitoring, alerting and notifications play a pivotal role in ensuring the continuous availability and reliability of services. Linkerd integrates with alert management systems to provide operators with timely notifications about critical service disruptions or performance anomalies within a service mesh.

Linkerd leverages Prometheus Alertmanager for alerting, which enables classification, routing, and notification based on user-defined rules. Alertmanager can be configured to send notifications to various endpoints, including email, Slack, PagerDuty, and other collaboration or incident management platforms.

The fundamental components of an alerting system involve the definition of alert rules in Prometheus. These rules evaluate real-time metrics collected by Prometheus to determine if conditions indicative of issues have been met. When conditions are satisfied, an alert is triggered.

```
groups:
  - name: linkerd.rules
    rules:
    - alert: HighLatency
      expr: histogram_quantile(0.95, rate(http_request_duration_seconds_bucket{job
          ="linkerd"}[5m])) > 0.5
      for: 5m
      labels:
        severity: critical
      annotations:
        summary: "High latency detected"
        description: "95th percentile latency is over 500ms for more than 5 minutes."
```

This YAML snippet illustrates an alert rule that triggers when the 95th percentile of HTTP request durations exceeds 500 milliseconds for more than five minutes. The rule specifies both a condition (latency threshold) and a duration, preventing transient issues from generating alerts. The labels categorize the alert's severity, while annotations provide context to aid operators in diagnosis.

Upon alert activation, Alertmanager handles the subsequent process, including:

- Deduplication: Suppresses duplicate alerts to reduce noise.

- Grouping: Bundles related alerts, streamlining communication and incident response.

- Routing: Directs alerts to the appropriate recipients or teams based on predefined configurations.

- Silencing: Temporarily mutes alerts for known issues or during scheduled maintenance.

Integrating Alertmanager with notification tools ensures that alerts are handled effectively and reach operators in a timely manner. Configuration for diverse notification channels is encapsulated in configuration files that define how and where alerts are to be sent:

```
receivers:
  - name: 'team-email'
    email_configs:
      - to: 'oncall@company.com'

  - name: 'pagerduty'
    pagerduty_configs:
```

## 7.3. ALERTING AND NOTIFICATIONS

```
      - routing_key: 'your-routing-key'
route:
  group_by: ['alertname']
  group_wait: 30s
  group_interval: 5m
  repeat_interval: 1h
  receiver: 'team-email'

inhibit_rules:
  - source_match:
      severity: 'critical'
    target_match:
      severity: 'warning'
    equal: ['alertname', 'service']
```

The configuration ensures that alerts are grouped by name, reducing the volume of notifications during simultaneous alert conditions, and specifies individual rules for alert routing and inhibition.

Effective alerting and notification systems require the fine-tuning of alert thresholds and conditions to minimize false positives and alert fatigue among operators. This balance ensures actionable alerts are prioritized, leading to faster detection and resolution of issues.

A successful alerting strategy with Linkerd involves continuous evaluation of alert rule performance and adapting configurations based on service behavior patterns, updates, or scaling activities:

- Adaptive Alerting: Dynamically adjusts thresholds based on anomalies detected using machine learning models or historical data patterns.

- Runbook Automation: Links alerts to predefined runbooks that outline necessary steps for incident resolution, leveraging automation where possible to expedite recovery processes.

- Notification Policies: Tailor notification strategies to align with the severity of the alert. Critical alerts may trigger immediate response protocols, while lower severity alerts can use less intrusive channels.

The implementation of alerting and notification mechanisms in Linkerd solidifies the service mesh's observability framework, ensuring operators can pre-emptively address potential disruptions before they impact users significantly. By facilitating real-time communication, these mechanisms empower operations teams to maintain the reliability, scalability, and efficiency of cloud-native applications.

## 7.4 Granular Observability with Prometheus

Monitoring and maintaining the health and performance of a service mesh requires a detailed and fine-grained approach to observability. Prometheus, with its robust capabilities for data collection and querying, provides granular observability by allowing deep insights into metrics at both the system and application levels in Linkerd.

Prometheus is an open-source systems monitoring and alerting toolkit widely known for its powerful time-series database, flexible query language (PromQL), and extensible platform architecture. In a Linkerd environment, Prometheus functions as the core observability tool, collecting metrics exported by Linkerd proxies and control plane components.

- **Collection of Fine-Grained Metrics**

Prometheus scrapes extensive metrics from Linkerd at regular intervals, enabling the observation of:

- **Traffic Metrics**: Metrics such as request rates, error rates, and response sizes provide insights into the traffic patterns and overall service utilization within the mesh.

- **Resource Usage Metrics**: Indicators like CPU usage, memory consumption, and network bandwidth usage aid in capacity planning and identifying inefficient resource utilization.

- **Latency Metrics**: Captures detailed latency information, including histograms and quantiles, which are crucial for detecting performance bottlenecks and understanding request flow dynamics.

## 7.4. GRANULAR OBSERVABILITY WITH PROMETHEUS

Linkerd exports its metrics in a Prometheus-readable format, typically as HTTP endpoints. These metrics are then automatically scraped by Prometheus based on the configured scrape_interval and metrics_path parameters, ensuring a consistent pipeline of up-to-date data.

```
scrape_configs:
 - job_name: 'linkerd'
   metrics_path: '/metrics'
   scheme: 'http'

   static_configs:
     - targets: ['l5d-proxy-1:4191', 'l5d-proxy-2:4191']
```

This YAML configuration illustrates a basic setup for scraping metrics from two Linkerd proxy instances, each exposed over HTTP at port 4191, the default for metrics.

- **Advanced Metrics Aggregation and Querying**

Prometheus's query language, PromQL, is tailor-made for operations on time-series data, offering the ability to execute sophisticated queries that can aggregate, slice, and dice the data for comprehensive analysis. PromQL supports operations such as sum, average, and quantiles, which empower users to generate actionable insights from raw metrics.

```
100 * sum(rate(http_requests_total{status=~"2.."}[5m]))
/ sum(rate(http_requests_total[5m]))
```

In this PromQL query, the success rate of requests is computed by dividing the sum rate of successful HTTP responses (2xx status codes) by the total number of requests over a sliding five-minute window. Such queries facilitate the monitoring of key performance indicators (KPIs) that are crucial to operations teams.

Beyond basic querying, Prometheus supports creating range vectors and instant vectors, which allow analyzing across time ranges to observe historical trends or instant snapshots for immediate assessments. This capability is beneficial for understanding the service behavior in retrospective analyses, which can guide decisions regarding infrastructure management and scaling activities.

- **Custom Metrics and Instrumentation**

While Linkerd provides a comprehensive set of default metrics, there are scenarios where custom application-specific metrics are necessary. Prometheus supports custom metrics collection, where developers can define and integrate specific metrics tailored to their application logic.

Applications running in a Linkerd mesh can be instrumented using client libraries available for various programming languages. These libraries facilitate the creation of custom time-series metrics, allowing enhanced observability over bespoke application behaviors, such as business transactions or specific algorithm performance.

```
from prometheus_client import start_http_server, Summary

# Create a metric to track request processing time
REQUEST_TIME = Summary('request_processing_seconds', 'Time spent processing
    request')

@REQUEST_TIME.time()
def process_request(request):
    # Simulate processing of the request
    time.sleep(2)

if __name__ == '__main__':
    start_http_server(8000)
    while True:
        process_request(None)
```

This Python example illustrates how to instrument a simple application with a custom metric tracking request processing time, exposing it on an HTTP server that Prometheus can scrape.

- **Deriving Insights through Dashboards**

Granular observability ensures that data is not only collected but is also presented in a way that is interpretable and actionable. Integrating Prometheus with dashboarding tools such as Grafana extends the ability to create rich visualizations, enabling quick assessments of the overall system state.

Grafana provides an enhanced user interface to build real-time, interactive dashboards that portray various metrics collected via Prometheus. Users can customize dashboards to visualize trends, anomalies, and projections, ensuring any service degradation is promptly identified and addressed.

Dashboarding supports multiple panel types, from simple graphs representing time-series data to complex status panels and heatmaps that show geographical or logical distribution of service components. The interactivity allows operations teams to drill down from high-level overviews to specific, granular details.

- **Continuous Improvement and Feedback Mechanisms**

Ensuring ongoing reliability and performance in a service mesh requires iterative improvements, informed by insights gleaned from comprehensive observability data. Prometheus analytics can be used to establish feedback loops for continuous improvement initiatives. Historical metrics data, trend analyses, and real-time monitoring contribute to informed decision-making processes, such as:

- **Automated Scaling**: Using historical usage patterns and real-time telemetry data to proactively scale services before demand outpaces capacity.

- **Anomaly Detection**: Implementing machine learning models on top of Prometheus metrics can enhance prediction and early detection mechanisms.

- **Incident Management**: Enabling retrospective incident analyses to ascertain root causes and prevent recurrence.

Linkerd's leverage of Prometheus for granular observability is quintessential for operating high-performance, scalable service mesh environments. The integration facilitates robust data collection, sophisticated querying, and versatile visualization capabilities that collectively underpin decision-making processes, operational efficiency, and ultimately the reliability and performance of modern cloud-native applications.

## 7.5 Visualizing Service Health with Grafana

Visualizing the health of services in a dynamic and distributed environment is crucial for effective operations and maintenance. Grafana, an open-source visualization and analytics software, plays a pivotal role in transforming raw metrics into comprehensible insights when integrated with Prometheus in a Linkerd-managed service mesh. This integration provides robust visualization capabilities that enhance observability, aid in the detection of anomalies, and support capacity planning and performance optimization.

Grafana's architecture is built around a model that emphasizes flexibility and extensibility, allowing users to create dashboards that are not only visually appealing but also highly functional. Its ability to connect to a wide array of data sources, including Prometheus, makes it an invaluable tool for monitoring complex service meshes orchestrated by Linkerd.

**Setting Up Grafana with Linkerd** To begin visualizing Linkerd's telemetry data using Grafana, the initial step is to integrate Grafana with the Prometheus instance collecting Linkerd metrics. The configuration involves setting up Prometheus as a data source in Grafana.

```
{
  "name": "Prometheus",
  "type": "prometheus",
  "access": "proxy",
  "url": "http://localhost:9090",
  "basicAuth": false,
  "isDefault": true
}
```

The JSON configuration above illustrates the process of adding Prometheus as a data source. The 'url' specifies where Prometheus is hosted, typically on port 9090, and other fields configure connection settings like authentication and access.

With Prometheus configured, Grafana can begin querying for metrics collected from Linkerd's proxies and control plane. These metrics form the foundation upon which dashboards are built.

**Designing Effective Grafana Dashboards** Grafana excels at presenting multi-faceted visualizations through its dashboard panels, which can represent different metric types and allow for dynamic interaction. An effective Grafana dashboard should be designed to convey critical information succinctly and intuitively, enabling

## 7.5. VISUALIZING SERVICE HEALTH WITH GRAFANA

operators to quickly discern the state and health of the services.

- **Time-Series Panels**: These are used to display data over time, showing trends and patterns. Common metrics viewed in time-series graphs include request rates, error counts, and latency timings. These panels show how these metrics evolve, helping to identify anomalies or shifts in performance.

- **Heatmaps**: Ideal for visualizing the distribution and density of data, heatmaps can be employed to show latency distributions across services, identifying outliers and helping to isolate inefficiencies.

- **Single Stat Panels**: These panels display a single aggregated value, such as the current number of active requests or the average CPU usage. Single stat panels provide at-a-glance information on critical resource consumption metrics.

- **Histogram Panels**: Useful for representing data distributions, histograms can be applied to latency data, showcasing percentile distributions or response time categorizations across services.

- **Alerts and Annotations**: Dashboards can include alerts and annotations for metrics that traverse predefined thresholds, highlighting potential issues requiring immediate attention.

An example configuration for a simple time-series panel to visualize HTTP request rates is shown below:

```
{
  "type": "graph",
  "title": "HTTP Request Rate",
  "targets": [
    {
      "expr": "sum(rate(http_requests_total[5m])) by (service)",
      "intervalFactor": 1,
      "legendFormat": "{{service}}"
    }
  ],
  "xaxis": {
    "mode": "time",
    "name": null,
    "show": true
  },
  "yaxes": [
    {
```

```
      "format": "short",
      "label": "Requests",
      "show": true
    }
  ]
}
```

This snippet configures a time-series graph to show HTTP request rates aggregated by service, providing quick visual feedback on traffic volumes.

**Advanced Grafana Features for Enhancing Observability**
Grafana's strength lies in its myriad features designed to enhance the monitoring experience:

- **Templating**: Use variables and templates to create dynamic dashboards that can adapt to different services, environments, or time ranges. This helps in reducing duplicate dashboards and allows for customizable views tailored to specific operational needs.

- **Annotations**: Operators can add annotations on graphs to mark events of interest, such as deployments or incidents. This contextual information aids in correlating changes in metrics with specific events in the service timeline.

- **Alert Management**: Grafana can be integrated with alert systems to notify operators via email, Slack, or other channels when certain thresholds are exceeded, facilitating quick response to developing issues.

- **Dashboard Sharing**: Grafana supports secure sharing of dashboards among teams, promoting collaborative review and analysis. Supporting features for snapshots and embedding aid in integrating visualizations directly into reports or external applications.

- **Panels Customization**: Users can customize nearly every aspect of a panel, from colors and formats to thresholds and legends, ensuring that dashboards align with organizational standards and preferences.

**Practical Benefits of Using Grafana for Linkerd Mesh** The combination of Linkerd and Grafana with Prometheus data leads to a number of practical benefits:

- **Improved Insight Into Dependencies**: By visualizing service interactions, teams gain a better understanding of how services interoperate, assisting in troubleshooting and root cause analysis.

- **Capacity Planning**: Identifying trends in resource utilization via Grafana allows teams to plan effectively for scaling operations and maintaining optimal performance levels.

- **Enhanced User Experience**: Continuous monitoring of service health helps maintain high availability and performance standards, directly impacting user satisfaction and application success.

- **Proactive Issue Resolution**: Graphical alerts and threshold-breach annotations allow teams to preemptively address potential issues before they affect end-users.

Integrating Grafana with Linkerd via Prometheus provides valuable visibility across the service mesh, transforming raw data into actionable insights. By enabling teams to efficiently monitor, alert, and respond to the dynamic conditions of distributed applications, Grafana serves as an indispensably powerful tool that optimizes both operational oversight and strategic insight.

## 7.6 Monitoring Service Dependencies

In a distributed system architecture, it is crucial to monitor and understand the dependencies between services. Service dependency monitoring is a vital aspect of maintaining system reliability and performance within a Linkerd service mesh, as it allows for proactive management of inter-service interactions and the early detection of potential failure points.

The complexity of service interactions in a microservices environment can be considerable, with each service potentially dependent on multiple others for data, processing, and functionality. This web of dependencies introduces challenges related to observability, troubleshooting, and latency management that can have profound impacts on service availability.

- **Service Dependency Concepts**: Service dependencies in a Linkerd mesh can be described as the set of relationships that exist between different services or components. These dependencies can be direct when a service calls another service's API, or indirect, exemplified by shared resources such as databases or message queues.

  Linkerd simplifies the process of dependency observability by leveraging its robust telemetry features, which include tracking traffic flows and collecting metrics across service boundaries. This telemetry forms the foundation for understanding how services depend on one another, enabling operators to map interactions and identify performance bottlenecks.

- **Tracking and Visualizing Dependencies**: Linkerd, when combined with a tracing tool like Jaeger or Zipkin and a metrics database like Prometheus, provides powerful tools for tracking service dependencies:

  - **Tracing**: As requests traverse between services, tracing allows capturing and correlating these interactions. By tagging requests with unique identifiers, it's possible to follow their path throughout the mesh, gaining insights into the latency and processing time at each step. This trace data can then be visualized to map out service interactions.

    ```
    {
      "traceId": "h1i2j3k4l5m6n7o8",
      "spans": [
        {
          "id": "aa11",
          "parentId": null,
          "name": "get /orders",
          "serviceName": "order-service",
          "startTime": 1677900000000,
          "duration": 350,
          "tags": {"component": "database-access"}
    ```

## 7.6. MONITORING SERVICE DEPENDENCIES

```
    },
    {
      "id": "bb22",
      "parentId": "aa11",
      "name": "call /inventory",
      "serviceName": "inventory-service",
      "startTime": 1677900000350,
      "duration": 150,
      "tags": {"component": "http"}
    }
  ]
}
```

In this example, a trace follows a request from an order-service to an inventory-service, depicting the hierarchical relationship and capturing timing metrics.

- **Metrics**: Prometheus metrics further delineate service dependencies by collecting detailed, time-series data. Useful metrics for dependency monitoring include error rates, request counts, and response times. Analyzing these metrics provides insight into the performance and availability of services as they interact.

```
sum(rate(http_requests_total{job="inventory-service", status
    !~"2.."}[1m]))
  / sum(rate(http_requests_total{job="inventory-service"}[1m]))
```

This PromQL query calculates the error rate for the inventory-service by evaluating non-2xx HTTP responses—a useful metric for assessing dependency impact.

- **Visualization Tools**: Visualization tools, such as Grafana, can represent these dependency mappings through dashboards that highlight key metrics like request latency distributions across services or dependency graphs that showcase inter-service calls.

- **Understanding and Managing Dependency Risks**: With dependencies mapped, the focus shifts to understanding and managing risks or challenges these dependencies pose. Some of the primary risks include:

  - **Cascading Failures**: A failure in one service can propagate across the mesh, causing dependent services to fail in turn. Monitoring allows detection of such patterns, and operators may apply techniques like circuit breakers and retries to mitigate this risk.

- **Latency Amplification**: The compounded latency as requests traverse multiple services can significantly impact response times. A solid monitoring strategy identifies where latencies accumulate, pinpointing bottlenecks in processing times.

- **Resource Saturation**: Traffic spikes can lead to resource bottlenecks in shared services, affecting their dependents. By tracking resource utilization and interaction patterns, operators can implement autoscaling and other resource management preemptively.

- **Building Resilient Service Dependencies**: The insights gained from robust dependency monitoring equip teams to build more resilient architectures. Several strategies can be employed:

  - **Redundancy and Failover**: Introduce redundancy in critical service paths, and design failover strategies to reroute traffic in case of service failures. Ensure critical services have backup instances or alternative pathways to maintain availability.

  - **Service Decomposition**: Re-evaluate tightly coupled services and consider decomposing them into smaller, independently deployable units to reduce the blast radius of any single failure.

  - **Dependency Injection**: Make use of dependency injection patterns to manage service interactions dynamically, allowing for easier testing and adaptation to new service versions.

  - **Chaos Engineering**: Practice chaos engineering to intentionally inject failures and stress scenarios into the system. This testing uncovers vulnerabilities in dependency chains and helps fine-tune failover strategies and recovery mechanisms.

- **Long-term Benefits of Dependency Monitoring**: Investing in comprehensive service dependency monitoring provides significant, long-term benefits including:

    - **Enhanced Operational Insight**: Operators gain a complete view of how services interoperate, simplifying root cause analysis and troubleshooting processes.
    - **Agility in Development**: Developers can iterate faster and with greater confidence, knowing the dependency relationships are transparent, monitored, and manageable.
    - **Customer Satisfaction**: By ensuring service reliability through proactive monitoring, operators can improve end-user experience, resulting in heightened customer satisfaction and loyalty.
    - **Cost Management**: Improved observability helps optimize resource allocation and service performance, leading to cost savings in cloud infrastructure and operational efforts.

Linkerd's capability to facilitate observing service dependencies transforms how modern applications are managed, ensuring they are not only robust and reliable, but also scalable to meet evolving business demands. Monitoring service dependencies isn't merely about identifying current states but is an essential process that supports ongoing improvement and resilience-building across the service mesh.

# Chapter 8

# Linkerd Performance and Scalability

Ensuring optimal performance and scalability is crucial for the effective operation of Linkerd within dynamic and growing environments. This chapter delves into strategies for optimizing Linkerd's configuration to handle high-performance demands efficiently. It explores techniques for both horizontal and vertical scaling, enabling the service mesh to manage increased loads effectively. The chapter also addresses resource management, providing insights into efficiently allocating and utilizing system resources. Additionally, best practices for performance benchmarking and testing are discussed to identify potential bottlenecks. Collectively, these elements equip users to enhance Linkerd's responsiveness and throughput, supporting seamless scalability and adaptation in production environments.

## 8.1 Optimizing Linkerd for High Performance

Optimizing Linkerd for high performance in varied deployment environments requires a detailed understanding of its configuration options and operational parameters. This section outlines strategies for fine-tuning Linkerd to function efficiently and deliver high throughput with minimal latency. By addressing critical resources, intelligently leveraging Linkerd features, and evaluating environmental factors, performance can be enhanced significantly.

Linkerd acts as a transparent, lightweight proxy running next to each service instance. Proper optimization involves adjustments both at the Linkerd level and in the surrounding infrastructure. We emphasize specific configurations, from low-level network tuning to high-level architectural changes, offering insights into how to implement them successfully.

The core areas that influence Linkerd's performance are efficient use of CPU and memory, effective network and traffic management, enhancing resilience through retries and timeouts, and appropriate configuration of Linkerd's control plane components. Each component must be considered to maximize Linkerd's performance in terms of response time and throughput.

### CPU and Memory Optimization

Linkerd's proxy, built on Rust, offers a highly efficient execution model. To optimize CPU and memory utilization, it is crucial to configure the resource allocations properly within Kubernetes. Establish explicit requests and limits to ensure the Linkerd proxy sidecar has sufficient resources. Recommended defaults are often a starting point, but tuning these values based on real usage patterns can offer significant gains.

```
resources:
  requests:
    cpu: "50m"
    memory: "64Mi"
  limits:
    cpu: "500m"
    memory: "256Mi"
```

## 8.1. OPTIMIZING LINKERD FOR HIGH PERFORMANCE

Monitoring CPU and memory usage over time is essential to ensure these settings align with performance goals. Prometheus, a widely used monitoring tool, facilitates this by collecting metrics from Linkerd's proxies and controllers.

```
- job_name: 'linkerd'
  scrape_interval: 15s
  static_configs:
    - targets: ['localhost:9990']
```

Adjust these intervals and thresholds based on the specific load and performance requirements.

## Network and Traffic Management

The role of networking in Linkerd optimization is significant. It maintains a fine balance between throughput (bandwidth), packet processing efficiency, and latency. Key configurations include adjusting the Maximum Transmission Unit (MTU) size for network packets, which can be crucial for overall data path efficiency.

To optimize MTU, first determine the optimal size for the network. Tools like 'iperf' can help evaluate network capacity and throughput to adjust configurations accordingly. Improper MTU settings may lead to packet fragmentation, reducing efficiency.

Moreover, configure connection pooling and keep-alive settings to reduce connection setup latency. These settings impact how long connections remain open and ready to serve subsequent requests. Below is an example of how these might be configured:

```
# Example on setting keep-alive for HTTP in application code
http.setKeepAliveTimeout(linger, TimeUnit.SECONDS);
http.setMaxKeepAliveRequests(maxRequests);
```

These settings help maintain open connections, reducing latency for recurring client requests.

## Control Plane Configuration

The Linkerd control plane is responsible for policy and configuration management and must be optimized to prevent it from becoming a bottleneck under load. The default configuration may not suffice for high-traffic environments, requiring custom tuning.

Ensure the control plane components are appropriately resourced, similar to the proxy, with correct CPU and memory requests and limits. Linkerd's control plane scalability depends on factors such as the number of Kubernetes objects it must manage and the frequency of changes.

Horizontal scaling of control plane components can increase fault tolerance and handle peak loads effectively. This can be achieved by deploying multiple replicas.

```
replicas: 3
```

This configuration leads to better load distribution among control plane instances, ensuring each accepts a manageable amount of load.

## Latency Optimization and Timeouts

In service meshes, reducing latency and properly setting timeouts can profoundly affect response times. Latency can be affected by the circuit breaker settings and the automatic retry mechanism that needs careful calibration.

```
linkerd2.autoRetries: 5
linkerd2.timeout: "30s"  # global timeouts
```

The retry mechanism adjusts how Linkerd handles failed requests, with an optimal configuration striking a balance between reliability and performance. Excessive retries may exacerbate issues during partial failure scenarios, leading to increased congestion. Understanding the failure domains and setting logical limits is critical.

The timeout settings should be consistent with the expected service response times to avoid unnecessary request cancelation. Comprehensive testing under various scenarios helps determine appropriate retry and timeout configurations.

## Profiling and Monitoring

Performance profiling and monitoring are paramount in identifying bottlenecks and ensuring optimal operational conditions. Advanced tracing tools, such as Jaeger or Zipkin, integrated with Prometheus metrics, enable a granular performance analysis.

Analyze latency histograms to identify specific queue lengths that delay request processing and pinpoint where high variability exists in service response times. Below is an example configuration for Jaeger integration:

```
tracing:
  enabled: true
  endpoint: "jaeger-collector:14268/api/traces"
  samplingRate: 0.1
```

Using a suitable sampling rate ensures tracing does not overburden the system while providing sufficient data for analysis.

## Scaling Strategies

Scale Linkerd components in response to deficient performance indicators. Effective use of both horizontal (replicas) and vertical (resource allocation) scaling can enhance resilience and performance. Utilize Kubernetes' Horizontal Pod Autoscaler (HPA) for proactive adjustments to workloads in real time.

```
apiVersion: autoscaling/v2beta2
kind: HorizontalPodAutoscaler
metadata:
  name: linkerd-controller
spec:
  scaleTargetRef:
    apiVersion: apps/v1
    kind: Deployment
    name: linkerd-controller
  minReplicas: 1
  maxReplicas: 10
  metrics:
  - type: Resource
    resource:
      name: cpu
      target:
        type: Utilization
        averageUtilization: 70
```

Implementing HPA ensures elasticity, promoting efficient use of resources under varying demand loads.

Optimizing Linkerd for high performance is a continuous process of tailoring and adjusting numerous variables according to observed behavior and traffic patterns. By methodically addressing aspects of resource allocation, networking, proxy configurations, and control plane processing, Linkerd can be tuned to meet rigorous performance requirements. These enhancements ensure scalability and robustness, crucial for seamless traffic handling in dynamic environments.

## 8.2 Horizontal and Vertical Scaling Techniques

Scaling is fundamental to ensuring that Linkerd can handle increasing loads and support seamless performance in diverse environments. The concepts of horizontal and vertical scaling provide the two principal methodologies for adjusting system resources to meet greater scale demands and ensure service reliability and efficiency.

Horizontal scaling—also known as scaling out—involves adding more instances or nodes to distribute the workload evenly across multiple units. This approach is ideal for accommodating increased load by multiplying the system's capacity and enhancing fault tolerance. Vertical scaling—scaling up—entails increasing the resources, such as CPU and memory, of existing nodes. This section examines how both techniques can be applied effectively within a Linkerd deployment.

Horizontal scaling in a Linkerd setup primarily involves the addition of pods or instances to manage traffic loads. Within Kubernetes, this is often achieved using the Horizontal Pod Autoscaler (HPA), which dynamically adjusts the number of pod replicas based on observed CPU utilization or other selected metrics, such as memory usage or custom metrics provided by tools like Prometheus.

To configure HPA for Linkerd, it starts with setting appropriate resource requests and limits on Linkerd deployments to ensure valid scaling decisions. Here's an example YAML HPA configuration:

```
apiVersion: autoscaling/v2beta2
```

## 8.2. HORIZONTAL AND VERTICAL SCALING TECHNIQUES

```
kind: HorizontalPodAutoscaler
metadata:
  name: linkerd-web
spec:
  scaleTargetRef:
    apiVersion: apps/v1
    kind: Deployment
    name: linkerd-web
  minReplicas: 1
  maxReplicas: 10
  metrics:
  - type: Resource
    resource:
      name: cpu
      target:
        type: Utilization
        averageUtilization: 50
```

This configuration results in the dynamic scaling of 'linkerd-web' deployment based on CPU usage, maintaining processor utilization around 50%. Notably, adjusting the 'minReplicas' and 'maxReplicas' fields adjust the auto-scaling boundaries.

The merits of horizontal scaling include redundancy and fault tolerance with the distribution of traffic across multiple pods, reducing single points of failure. Additionally, it allows for more manageable incremental adjustments to capacity aligned with traffic patterns.

When implementing horizontal scaling, several considerations must be accounted for to avoid common pitfalls:

- **Load Balancing**: Ensure that the load is evenly distributed among instances. Kubernetes provides a native load balancing mechanism that accompanies horizontal scaling. It is important to review and potentially tune these settings to perform optimally under scaled conditions.

- **State Management**: Stateless services are more suitable for horizontal scaling. If Linkerd manages states, strategies such as shared state stores or session stickiness might be necessary.

- **Consistency and Data Integrity**: Distributed systems often face challenges related to consistency; hence, ensuring data integrity with techniques like consensus algorithms or eventual consistency models is advised.

- **Network Latency**: As services scale horizontally, minimize intra-cluster traffic latencies through well-architected service placements and geographic considerations.

- **Scaling Latency**: Evaluate the lag between decision and effect in HPA adjustments to prevent underscaling during traffic spikes and overscaling during quiet periods.

Vertical scaling complements horizontal scaling by enhancing the capacity and performance of individual nodes or pods. In Kubernetes-based deployments, vertical scaling involves increasing the resources available to pods through resource quota adjustments.

It begins with defining resource requests and limits appropriately, scaling up as necessary based on benchmarking and monitoring insights. An example deployment configuration with updated resource specs might look like this:

```
apiVersion: apps/v1
kind: Deployment
metadata:
  name: linkerd-proxy
spec:
  template:
    spec:
      containers:
      - name: linkerd-proxy
        resources:
          requests:
            cpu: "200m"
            memory: "256Mi"
          limits:
            cpu: "1000m"
            memory: "1Gi"
```

The configuration outlines new CPU and memory settings for a 'linkerd-proxy' pod, effectively enhancing its capacity to process more requests concurrently.

While vertical scaling can immediately improve performance without architectural overhauls, it bears limitations such as:

- **Physical Hardware Constraints**: Eventually, physical hardware limits resource increases. Over-dependence on vertical scaling may lead to diminishing returns—certain subjective to Moore's Law patterns.

## 8.2. HORIZONTAL AND VERTICAL SCALING TECHNIQUES

- **Downtime Risks**: Though Kubernetes updates can be executed with minimal downtime through rolling updates, significant resource alterations may necessitate momentary service disruption.

- **Cost Efficiency**: Larger instance types are typically more expensive than smaller ones per resource unit. Budget considerations thus play a pivotal role in deciding scaling strategy.

- **Overall Fault Tolerance Reduction**: Unlike horizontal scaling, vertical strategies do not inherently provide increased fault tolerance.

Effective scaling strategies hinge on robust monitoring and performance analysis. Tools like Prometheus integrated with Grafana visualize metrics and thresholds that guide scaling decisions. Here is a sample configuration for Prometheus to collect and monitor CPU and memory utilization metrics.

```
global:
  scrape_interval: 15s
scrape_configs:
 - job_name: 'linkerd'
   static_configs:
    - targets: ['localhost:9990']
```

Prometheus's 'alertmanager' facilitates proactive alert setup based on detected metric anomalies like CPU spikes, enabling timely scaling interventions.

Integrating tracing with tools such as Jaeger gives visibility into request paths and latencies, offering indicators of capacity limits before stress arises.

Deciding when to use horizontal versus vertical scaling depends on the specific architecture, workload, and cost-benefit analysis. Generally, horizontal scaling is ideal for microservices environments emphasizing elasticity and fault tolerance. It supports distributed workloads in cloud-native architectures, encouraging redundancy.

Vertical scaling, when workloads are monolithic or when immediate equipment constraints pose challenges, serves best as a temporary solution. It's optimal for scenarios where licensing restricts instance counts or where applications lack distributed design suitability.

In practice, a hybrid approach frequently yields the most balanced outcomes. For example:

- Utilize vertical scaling initially for rapid adjustments.

- Implement horizontal scaling for longer-term load adjustments as demand stabilizes.

- Monitor continuously for capacity changes, fine-tuning limits based on evolving demand patterns.

By integrating horizontal and vertical scaling with monitoring, performance profiling, and environment-specific constraints, administrations can tailor strategies that support service reliability, robustness, and efficiency while optimizing operational costs. These techniques together safeguard Linkerd's operational integrity as it scales to meet user demand variably and sustainably.

## 8.3 Resource Management and Quotas

Efficient resource management and the strategic use of quotas are pivotal to maintaining Linkerd's performance and ensuring that the system can reliably handle varying loads without compromising service quality. This section explores the principles and best practices for resource allocation, applying quotas effectively within Kubernetes, and optimizing Linkerd's components to avert resource contention and achieve seamless operation.

At the heart of resource management is the understanding of compute, memory, and network resources' roles within a Kubernetes cluster. The orchestration of these resources, especially concerning Linkerd's service mesh requirements, determines the system's flexibility and resilience under load stresses.

- **Understanding Resource Types**

Resources in Kubernetes, and by extension in Linkerd setups, are generally categorized into CPU, memory, and ephemeral storage. Here's a detailed examination and management strategy for each:

## 8.3. RESOURCE MANAGEMENT AND QUOTAS

- **CPU**: Measured in millicores, CPU resources determine the computation power available to pods. A comprehensive understanding of baseline and peak CPU usage informs correct allocation and request settings to ensure no service interruption.

- **Memory**: Indicated in bytes, this dictates the data volume a pod can handle. Surpassing limits leads to OutOfMemory (OOM) errors, prompting the need for strategic memory usage analysis.

- **Ephemeral Storage**: Although not extensively discussed here, ephemeral storage accommodates temporary data needs, including logs and caches, relevant in high I/O operations.

- **Resource Requests and Limits Configuration**

Proper configuration of resource requests and limits forms the core strategy of Kubernetes' resource management, determining how resources are allocated to pods and gauging clusters' overall utilization:

- **Requests** determine the resources guaranteed to a pod.
- **Limits** signify the maximal resources permissible for use by a pod, preventing a single container from consuming excess resources.

Here is an example of setting requests and limits for a Linkerd proxy within a Kubernetes deployment:

```
apiVersion: apps/v1
kind: Deployment
metadata:
  name: linkerd-proxy
spec:
  template:
    spec:
      containers:
      - name: linkerd-proxy
        resources:
          requests:
            cpu: "100m"
            memory: "128Mi"
          limits:
            cpu: "500m"
            memory: "256Mi"
```

In this configuration:

- **CPU Requests** are set to 100 millicores, guaranteeing the Linkerd proxy a baseline computation capacity.

- **Memory Requests** ensure the proxy gets 128 MiB, sufficient for expected workload.

- **Limits** are marginally higher for both CPU and memory, accommodating unforeseen spikes without impacting the cluster's stability.

Such configurations should be adjusted based on profiling data obtained from monitoring tools like Prometheus, which can reveal patterns in resource usage.

- **Implementing Resource Quotas**

Resource quotas act as an essential management tool that Kubernetes provides to control aggregate resource allocation per namespace. They ensure that no single namespace monopolizes resources to the detriment of others. These quotas enforce restrictions on the number of resources a namespace can consume, including CPU, memory, and storage.

Below is a YAML configuration example implementing resource quotas:

```
apiVersion: v1
kind: ResourceQuota
metadata:
  name: compute-resources
  namespace: linkerd-ns
spec:
  hard:
    requests.cpu: "4"
    requests.memory: "4Gi"
    limits.cpu: "10"
    limits.memory: "10Gi"
```

This defines a quota named 'compute-resources' in the 'linkerd-ns' namespace, setting hard caps on the requests and limits for CPU and memory resources.

The significance of establishing resource quotas lies in:

## 8.3. RESOURCE MANAGEMENT AND QUOTAS

- **Promoting Fairness**: Ensuring diverse workloads receive appropriate resources proportionately enhances service reliability across multiple applications.
- **Avoiding Starvation**: Prevents any single namespace from exhausting shared resources critical to other services.
- **Budgeting and Planning**: Facilitates predictable resource allocation aligned with organizational goals and budgets.

Quotas should be dynamically adjusted to reflect changing demand patterns, maintaining synergy between system growth and capacity.

- **Monitoring Resource Utilization**

Effective real-time monitoring of resource utilization is a prerequisite for optimized resource management. By leveraging monitoring solutions such as Prometheus and Grafana, operators can gather metrics on resource usage across Linkerd services.

```
- job_name: 'node'
  static_configs:
  - targets:
    - 'localhost:9100'
# Sample metric retrieval in PromQL
rate(container_cpu_usage_seconds_total{pod_name=~"linkerd.*"}[5m])
```

The job configuration collects node-level metrics, while the PromQL query retrieves the rate of CPU usage for pods prefixed with "linkerd". The dynamic dashboarding capabilities of Grafana allow for visualization of these metrics, exposing anomalies or inefficiencies in resource consumption.

- **Best Practices for Optimizing Linkerd Resource Usage**

To manage resources proficiently, the following best practices should be considered:

- **Routine Benchmarking**: Regular performance benchmarking of Linkerd components ensures insight into resource needs and identifies areas for possible improvements.

- **Profiling Workloads**: Detailed understanding of workload resource consumption sequences helps tailor deployment-specific optimizations.

- **Gradual Resource Adjustments**: Employ incremental changes to requests and limits, enabling clear visibility into the impact of scaling operations.

- **Dependency Management**: Properly manage third-party dependencies that could influence resource consumption unpredictably.

- **Granular Monitoring Alerts**: Implement alerts on real-time data monitoring dashboards, enabling preemptive interventions before potential resource exhaustion.

- **Adaptive Quota Policies**: Reevaluate resource quota policies periodically, adjusting for growth trends and new service introductions.

Balancing resource management and quotas effectively supports Linkerd's scalable operations without exceeding allocated capacities. Maintaining an adaptable and loading analysis framework enables prompt adaptation to diverse workloads, keeping resource usage within prescribed limits while delivering high-quality service.

## 8.4 Handling Large Scale Deployments

Handling large-scale deployments with Linkerd in dynamic environments requires strategic planning, precise execution, and ongoing maintenance. As deployments grow in size, numerous challenges arise, from maintaining consistent service availability and performance to managing the complexity and overhead introduced by vast service mesh architectures.

This section outlines comprehensive strategies for managing Linkerd in large-scale settings, covering essential practices that ensure effective service operation, scaling, observability, configuration, and networking within extensive clusters. Focus is laid on reliability, scalability, and security concerns that accompany the scaling of a service mesh.

## 8.4. HANDLING LARGE SCALE DEPLOYMENTS

- **Cluster Architecture and Design**

  Architecting a Kubernetes cluster for large-scale Linkerd deployments requires foresight into resource requirements and networking configurations. Designing an effective architecture means balancing resource use while ensuring that each layer of the cluster remains responsive under load.

  - **Node Profusion**: Large clusters typically entail numerous nodes, necessitating efficient load balancing and management across nodes. Proper distribution of pods ensures even resource use.
  - **High Availability**: Nodes and services must be replicated across availability zones to prevent downtime when a single node or zone fails.
  - **Multi-Cluster Setups**: Often, large deployments extend beyond a single cluster due to regional considerations or workload distribution needs, integrating multiple clusters seamlessly into a federated system.

  Here's a simplified example configuration for a multi-cluster federation:

  ```
  apiVersion: core.linkerd.io/v1alpha1
  kind: ServiceCluster
  metadata:
    name: secondary-cluster
  spec:
    kubeconfigSecret:
      name: secondary-cluster-kubeconfig
      namespace: linkerd-multicluster
  ```

  This configuration highlights a linked secondary cluster for load distribution and redundancy.

- **Configuration Management**

  Configuration management becomes increasingly critical as deployments grow. To handle these scenarios adeptly:

  - **GitOps Approach**: Implement a GitOps strategy where configurations are version-controlled, enabling quick rollbacks and consistent state management across environments.

- **Centralized Management Tools**: Use tools like Helm for templating complex configurations and maintaining uniformity across clusters.

  ```
  helm upgrade --install linkerd2 linkerd/linkerd2 --values=values.yaml
  ```

  This command uses Helm to apply changes across a cluster, ensuring configurations remain in sync.

- **Automated CI/CD Pipelines**: Establish CI/CD frameworks fostering rapid deployment and validation cycles, minimizing manual intervention and error potential.

• **Resource Efficiency and Scalability**

Resource efficiency in Linkerd must scale proportionally as deployments enlarge. The correlation between network and compute resources narrows with greater loads. Techniques for enhancing resource efficiency include:

- **Intelligent Resource Allocation**: Continuously evaluate and adjust Linkerd's deployment resource requests and limits to match the demand curve closely.

- **Adaptable Autoscaling Policies**: Implement both Horizontal Pod Autoscaler (HPA) and Vertical Pod Autoscaler (VPA) in tandem to encode flexible scaling logic accommodating unexpected demand variations.

- **Efficient Memory Management**: In persistent high-load scenarios, optimize the memory footprint through resource profiling and careful management of memory allocation per pod.

```
apiVersion: autoscaling/v2beta2
kind: HorizontalPodAutoscaler
metadata:
  name: linkerd-spike
spec:
  scaleTargetRef:
    apiVersion: apps/v1
    kind: Deployment
    name: linkerd-spike
  minReplicas: 1
  maxReplicas: 20
  metrics:
  - type: Pods
```

## 8.4. HANDLING LARGE SCALE DEPLOYMENTS

```
pods:
  metric:
    name: concurrentRequests
  target:
    type: AverageValue
    averageValue: 50
```

This HPA setup scales pods according to the 'concurrentRequests' metric, reflecting an adaptive scaling model high-performing in large deployments.

- **Networking Complexity and Optimization**

  Networking within extensive Linkerd deployments can pose significant bottlenecks if not diligently managed. Effective strategies include:

  - **Service Mesh Compression**: Leverage compression algorithms to minimize payload sizes traveling within the mesh, enhancing throughput.
  - **Locality-aware Service Placement**: Optimize service placement relative to requesting clients to reduce latency and enhance network bandwidth usage.
  - **Mesh Partitioning**: Componentize and partition the mesh where applicable, isolating high-traffic flows and containing failure domains.

```
apiVersion: proxy.linkerd.io/v1alpha1
kind: TrafficSplit
metadata:
  name: example-split
spec:
  service: my-service
  backends:
  - service: my-service-v1
    weight: 80
  - service: my-service-v2
    weight: 20
```

The TrafficSplit configurations distribute network requests efficiently across service versions, balancing load and enhancing network handling dynamically.

- **Observability and Monitoring**

Observability plays a vital role in large-scale operational readiness, capturing system intelligence essential for troubleshooting and optimization:

- **Integrative Monitoring Platforms**: Use Prometheus and Grafana to monitor mesh-wide and per-component level metrics, creating dashboards that highlight system health indicators clearly.
- **Distributed Tracing Solutions**: Implement distributed tracing systems like Jaeger to visualize the journey of each request across services, pinpointing latencies or misconfigurations.
- **Log Aggregation**: Centralize log collection using tools like Elasticsearch, Logstash, and Kibana (ELK stack) to analyze system performance trends and identify anomalies.

```
fluentd:
  enabled: true
elasticsearch:
  host: ${ELASTICSEARCH_HOST}
  port: 9200
```

This configuration enables Fluentd for log forwarding to an Elasticsearch deployment, promoting a unified view of logs across services.

- **Ensuring Service Reliability**

Reliability in large-scale deployments is preeminently addressed through:

- **Highly Redundant Design**: Deploy microservices redundantly, minimizing single points of failure across availability zones or regions.
- **Proactive Scalability**: Adopt pre-emptive scaling strategies accounting for forecasted demand, avoiding latency peaks that arise from reactive scaling mechanisms.
- **Cascading Failure Prevention**: Design systems with circuit breakers and fault-tolerant patterns to contain failures and prevent systemic outages.

```
{
    "service": "linkerd-svc",
    "circuit_breaker": {
        "enabled": true,
        "failRatio": 0.2,
        "timeout": 10
    }
}
```

Setting a circuit breaker mitigates risks associated with cascading failures, capping request failures within tolerable ratios and activating fallback processes.

The outlined strategies for managing Linkerd in expansive deployments provide a comprehensive guide to sustaining scalable, resilient, and optimized service operations. The integration of robust architectural design, resource management, meticulous networking orchestration, and comprehensive observability establishes a solid foundation for handling the complex challenges large-scale environments present. Through innovation and strategic planning, these principles enable seamless growth and efficient operation of ever-expanding Linkerd meshes.

## 8.5 Performance Benchmarking and Testing

Performance benchmarking and testing are integral to optimizing Linkerd deployments, ensuring that the service mesh can handle intended workloads efficiently and meet desired service levels. As systems scale and evolve, understanding the performance characteristics of Linkerd becomes essential to anticipate bottlenecks, ensure reliability, and maintain an optimal user experience.

This section explores methodologies for effective performance benchmarking and testing, focusing on designing test scenarios, selecting appropriate metrics, and utilizing tools to provide actionable insights. It underscores the importance of iterative testing to capture nuance in performance dynamics and the impact of configurational changes.

Benchmarking begins with defining the key parameters and environmental settings to test. This includes determining factors such as load levels, concurrency, and content types delivered through the mesh. A comprehensive benchmarking framework should include:

- **Test Environment Setup**: A closely mirrored production environment—ensure that configurations, versions, and datasets match closely to what is running in the production setting.

- **Baseline Establishment**: Conduct baseline measurements capturing the current performance metrics. This helps in quantifying improvements post-optimizations.

- **Metric Selection**: Determine performance metrics crucial to your use case including latency, throughput, error rate, and resource usage. These metrics provide insights into where bottlenecks may exist.

- **Testing Tools**: Selection of tools appropriate for load generation and metric collection. These may include specialized performance testing utilities like `wrk`, `JMeter`, or platform-specific integrations.

Designing load tests that mimic real-world scenarios is critical for providing meaningful insights into system behavior. Considerations in load test design should include:

- **Workload Modeling**: Simulate traffic patterns, peak loads, and concurrent user access levels. Modeling should reflect both average and extreme usage scenarios.

- **End-to-End System Testing**: Include tests that traverse multiple services within the mesh to understand holistic system impact. This captures interactions within the service mesh beyond isolated service metrics.

- **Gradual Load Increase**: Implement strategies such as stepped load tests that gradually increase the load, identifying thresholds beyond which performance degrades.

Here is a basic `wrk` load test command for generating HTTP requests at a specified rate:

## 8.5. PERFORMANCE BENCHMARKING AND TESTING

```
wrk -t12 -c400 -d30s http://linkerd-service.local
```

This command launches a load test with 12 threads and 400 connections directed at the linkerd-service.local endpoint for 30 seconds.

Post-test analysis of collected metrics is pivotal to identifying strengths and weaknesses in Linkerd's performance. Focal points include:

- **Response Times**: Analyze latency percentiles (e.g., 95th, 99th percentile) to understand worst-case response scenarios. Outliers in response times can suggest caching inefficiencies or resource blockages.

- **Throughput Analysis**: Examine data volume processed within specific durations, correlating throughput with stability under varying conditions.

- **Resource Utilization**: Observe CPU and memory utilization trends, enabling adjustments in resource requests and limits within your Kubernetes configurations.

Prometheus and Grafana dashboards can visualize these statistics, highlighting patterns that inform configuration tuning decisions.

```
- alert: HighRequestLatency
  expr: histogram_quantile(0.99, sum(rate(http_request_duration_seconds_bucket[5m
    ])) by (le)) > 0.5
  for: 2m
  labels:
    severity: 'warning'
  annotations:
    summary: "High request latency detected"
```

The Prometheus alert definition tracks latency breaches, alerting once the 99th percentile exceeds 500ms over a 5-minute window.

Beyond standard load tests, stress testing reveals system limits and robustness in response to unusual conditions:

- **Capacity Limits**: Stress tests help discern the maximum processing capacity of Linkerd before service degradation or failure, exposing scaling limits.

- **Fault Injection**: Introduce controlled failures, such as node failures or network partitioning. Tools like Gremlin or service mesh capabilities allow for scenario-based robustness testing.

- **Long-duration Tests**: Conduct prolonged test cycles covering extended operational periods. This can reveal memory leaks or resource exhaustion over time.

Example of injecting network latency using tc command:

```
tc qdisc add dev eth0 root netem delay 100ms
```

The above command introduces a 100ms delay on the network to simulate slowness or congestion.

Implementing an iterative approach to testing and optimization yields continuous enhancements to system performance. Key principles include:

- **Feedback Loops**: Establish feedback loops incorporating test outcomes into planning and optimization phases, ensuring a dynamic, responsive system evolution.

- **Continuous Integration (CI) Pipelines**: Integrate performance tests into CI pipelines. Automated testing enforces performance baselines whenever code or configuration changes occur.

- **Incremental Changes**: Initiate small configuration adjustments, scaling parameters iteratively to gauge their performance impact accurately.

```
kubectl apply -f updated-resource-config.yaml
kubectl rollout status deployment/linkerd
```

The above commands facilitate code pushes and ensure deployment readiness post-adjustments, fostering a cycle of continuous improvements.

The selection of performance testing tools must align with the testing objectives and infrastructure:

- **Web Performance Tools**: Use k6, JMeter, or wrk for HTTP-based traffic generation within the mesh.

- **A/B Testing Frameworks**: Employ A/B testing to compare configuration sets, authoritatively refining service mesh behavior based on experiential data.

- **Observability Infrastructures**: Leverage OpenTelemetry for detailed tracing analyses that complement monitoring, amplifying the understanding of request flows.

Benchmarking and testing are dynamic processes within any robust Linkerd deployment strategy. By implementing comprehensive testing methodologies that leverage scenario-based evaluations, utilize cutting-edge tools, and emphasize data-driven optimizations, operators are equipped to meet performance expectations consistently. These practices underpin Linkerd's ability to manage diverse, demanding workloads within modern microservices architectures.

## 8.6 Improving Response Times and Throughput

Enhancing response times and throughput in Linkerd deployments is imperative for delivering efficient service interactions and maintaining high-quality user experiences. Achieving these improvements necessitates a deep dive into the architecture and operational patterns of Linkerd, followed by strategic optimizations in configuration, resource allocation, and data flow management.

This section elaborates on methodologies to optimize response times and augment throughput. It addresses architectural adjustments, application-layer optimizations, network tuning, and system resource enhancements, underpinning the comprehensive approach needed for impactful performance improvement.

### Architecture and Configuration Optimization

The architecture within which Linkerd operates plays a fundamental role in impacting latency and throughput. Key adjustments may include:

- **Load Balancer Optimization**: Ensure that load balancing configurations optimize request distribution. Employ advanced strategies like Least Connections and Round Robin, considering compatibility with underlying infrastructure and workload specifics.

- **Decreasing Proxy Overhead**: Adjust settings of the Linkerd data plane proxies to minimize latency. This might involve optimizing keep-alive settings, connection pooling, and adjusting timeout configurations.

```
spec:
  template:
    metadata:
      annotations:
        config.linkerd.io/keep-alive: "true"
        config.linkerd.io/keep-alive-timeout: "10s"
```

This YAML snippet ensures that connections are persistently open, thereby reducing latency induced by TCP handshakes.

- **Namespace and Service Segmentation**: Organize services and workloads into logical namespaces and service groupings to enhance traffic manageability and reduce inter-service latency.

**Application-Layer Optimizations**

Improving performance at the application layer may involve both inter-service communication enhancements and application logic optimizations:

1. **HTTP/2 Utilization**: Linkerd supports HTTP/2, enabling multiplexed streams and reducing connection overhead. Ensure all relevant service paths are configured to leverage HTTP/2, particularly beneficial for high throughput services.

2. **Caching Strategies**: Implement local and edge caching mechanisms for repeat data requests. Caches reduce repetitive fetch requests, easing the load on back-end services.

```
app.use('/static', express.static('public', { maxAge: '1d' }));
```

The code sets caching headers for static assets, significantly enhancing response times for frequently requested content.

## 8.6. IMPROVING RESPONSE TIMES AND THROUGHPUT

3. **Batch Operations**: Where applicable, convert multiple small operations into batch requests, thus reducing request overheads.

```
List<Item> items = itemService.fetchItemsAsBatch(itemIds);
```

Batch-fetching items reduces transactional overhead and batching across the application layer fortifies throughput.

### Network Layer Tuning

Optimizing the network layer to reduce latency and enhance throughput remains critical:

- **MTU (Maximum Transmission Unit) Optimization**: Correctly configuring MTU can prevent packet fragmentation, reducing retransmits that lead to latency spikes.

```
ip link set dev eth0 mtu 1460
```

Adjust the MTU value optimistically according to the network's needs to keep fragmentation negligible.

- **TLS Performance Optimization**: Security mechanisms like TLS can add overhead; utilize SSL session reuse, optimized cipher suites, and hardware acceleration to reduce delay.

```
SSLContext sslContext = SSLContextBuilder.create().setProtocol("TLSv1
    .3").build();
```

The code outlines configuring SSL contexts with optimal TLS protocols, reducing handshake latency.

- **Traffic Compression**: Enable compression headers like Content-Encoding: gzip when applicable, decreasing data transmission sizes traversing the network.

### Enhancing System Resources

Efficient use of system resources significantly reduces both average and tail latency, boosting throughput:

1. **Efficient Resource Allocation**: Tune CPU and memory allocations to mitigate resource bottlenecks during peak loads. Observability tools like Prometheus can highlight potential overutilization or resource starvation events.

2. **Container Optimization**: Favor lightweight container images and leverage multi-stage builds to minimize container startup times and resource demands.

   ```
   FROM golang:alpine AS build
   WORKDIR /src
   COPY . .
   RUN CGO_ENABLED=0 GOOS=linux go build -o /app

   FROM scratch
   COPY --from=build /app /app
   ENTRYPOINT ["/app"]
   ```

   A multi-stage Dockerfile that efficiently builds lightweight Go binaries reducing container runtime overheads.

3. **Auto-Scaling Mechanisms**: Implement adaptive scaling policies with Kubernetes' Horizontal or Vertical Pod Autoscalers to match resource levels with demand gracefully, avoiding under-provisioning or overexpenditure of resources.

   ```
   apiVersion: autoscaling/v2beta2
   kind: HorizontalPodAutoscaler
   metadata:
     name: linkerd-scalable
   spec:
     scaleTargetRef:
       apiVersion: apps/v1
       kind: Deployment
       name: linkerd-scalable-deployment
     minReplicas: 2
     maxReplicas: 15
     metrics:
     - type: Resource
       resource:
         name: cpu
         target:
           type: Utilization
           averageUtilization: 60
   ```

   This HPA definition supports dynamic scaling to align demand and supply while improving responsiveness.

## Observability and Feedback Loops

Maintaining an elegant feedback loop from monitoring metrics to performance optimization measures enables informed corrections:

- **Implement Comprehensive Observability Dashboards**: Utilize Grafana to visualize latency, throughput, and resource

## 8.6. IMPROVING RESPONSE TIMES AND THROUGHPUT

utilization metrics holistically. Interactive dashboards facilitate real-time decision-making.

- **Establishing Alert Systems**: Define thresholds in Prometheus that trigger alerts when performance degrades or resources approach exhaustion.

```
- alert: HighCpuUsage
    expr: sum(rate(container_cpu_usage_seconds_total[5m])) by (pod) > 0.8
    for: 5m
    labels:
       severity: critical
    annotations:
       summary: "CPU usage is critically high"
```

The alert configuration signals excessive CPU usage, guiding preemptive scaling or optimization interventions.

By adopting a comprehensive approach to improve Linkerd response times and throughput, encompassing architectural efficiencies, application layer enhancements, and network optimizations, systems can be strategically positioned for performance excellence. Continuous monitoring and iteration ensure that deployments maintain scale and efficiency over time. These techniques not only fortify user experience through agile, responsive services but also amplify infrastructure potential, ensuring Linkerd's foundational support for evolving workloads.

Chapter 9

# Best Practices for Linkerd in Production

Implementing Linkerd in production environments requires adherence to best practices to ensure reliability and efficiency. This chapter provides key recommendations for preparing and deploying Linkerd at scale, emphasizing secure configuration and management of secrets. It discusses high availability strategies, including redundant deployments and failover mechanisms. Integration with continuous integration and deployment (CI/CD) systems is explored to streamline updates and rollouts. The chapter highlights the importance of establishing robust monitoring and incident response plans, as well as implementing backup and disaster recovery solutions. These practices collectively support the stability and resilience of Linkerd in production settings.

## 9.1 Preparing for Production Deployment

Deploying Linkerd in a production environment demands a comprehensive plan that addresses both the technical and operational facets of service management. By understanding the myriad of elements involved, teams can bring greater efficiency, reliability, and resilience to their cloud-native applications. This section meticulously examines the key considerations and essential steps required to ensure that Linkerd is primed for a smooth and effective production deployment.

The foundation of any successful deployment begins with a deep understanding of Linkerd's architectural components and how they are configured and interact within your Kubernetes cluster. Each component plays a pivotal role in how Linkerd functions. Therefore, before advancing to a production deployment, it is crucial to ensure that all configurations reflect the desired state of the system tailored to the specific business requirements.

**Networking and Cluster Setup**

A fundamental aspect of preparing Linkerd for production is the network topology and cluster configuration. Linkerd relies on the Kubernetes networking model to route traffic between services efficiently. Prior to deployment, consider the latency, bandwidth, and security implications of your cluster's network configuration. Ensure that your cluster has a robust networking layer capable of sustaining the traffic loads expected in production.

In Kubernetes, network policy configurations can help restrict traffic flow between services, adhering to the principle of least privilege. Proper implementation of network policies ensures that Linkerd can forward traffic appropriately while maintaining strict security controls.

```
apiVersion: networking.k8s.io/v1
kind: NetworkPolicy
metadata:
  name: allow-linkerd
spec:
  podSelector:
    matchLabels:
      app: linkerd
  ingress:
  - from:
```

## 9.1. PREPARING FOR PRODUCTION DEPLOYMENT

```
- namespaceSelector:
    matchLabels:
      name: linkerd
```

This policy allows ingress traffic only from the namespace housing Linkerd components, isolating control plane operations from other workloads.

### Resource Allocation and Scalability

Resource allocation is paramount in planning your production deployment. Linkerd's control plane components, such as the proxy injector, controller, and identity, require appropriate CPU and memory resources. Adequate resource allocation ensures that these components can fulfill their roles without bottlenecks. Implement horizontal or vertical pod autoscaling techniques to handle variable loads efficiently.

Use Kubernetes's horizontal pod autoscaler (HPA) to dynamically adjust the number of replicas based on CPU utilization or other custom metrics:

```
apiVersion: autoscaling/v2beta1
kind: HorizontalPodAutoscaler
metadata:
  name: linkerd-controller
spec:
  scaleTargetRef:
    apiVersion: apps/v1
    kind: Deployment
    name: linkerd-controller
  minReplicas: 2
  maxReplicas: 10
  metrics:
  - type: Resource
    resource:
      name: cpu
      targetAverageUtilization: 50
```

This configuration ensures that additional replicas of the Linkerd controller are deployed as CPU usage escalates, contributing to sustained performance during peak loads.

### Security Considerations

Security is a multi-layered aspect that begins with the control plane's integrity and extends to the data plane. Before deploying Linkerd in production, validate that the latest security patches are applied and that the configurations align with best practices. Embed strong authentication and authorization mechanisms using Kubernetes-native RBAC or mTLS to secure inter-component communication.

```
apiVersion: rbac.authorization.k8s.io/v1
kind: RoleBinding
metadata:
  name: linkerd-admin
roleRef:
  apiGroup: rbac.authorization.k8s.io
  kind: ClusterRole
  name: linkerd-admin
subjects:
- kind: User
  name: admin
  apiGroup: rbac.authorization.k8s.io
```

Incorporate regular vulnerability assessments to identify and swiftly mitigate any potential threats that could compromise the service mesh.

**Configuration Management and Version Control**

Configuration management emerges as a critical factor. Use tools such as ConfigMaps and Helm charts for managing configurations reliably, leveraging Git-based systems for version control. Document all configuration changes meticulously to maintain transparency and aid in troubleshooting.

```
apiVersion: v1
kind: ConfigMap
metadata:
  name: linkerd-config
  namespace: linkerd
data:
  proxy-log-level: info
  outbound-idle-timeout: 15m
```

This ConfigMap demonstrates how operational parameters can be dynamically managed without directly modifying the codebase.

**Testing and Quality Assurance**

Embedding rigorous testing in the deployment pipeline minimizes the likelihood of errors. Deploy Linkerd to a staging environment mirroring production to verify its behavior under realistic conditions, including load and stress testing.

Integrate end-to-end testing in CI/CD pipelines with tools like linkerd-check to detect potential conflicts or degradations before they reach production.

## 9.1. PREPARING FOR PRODUCTION DEPLOYMENT

```
$ linkerd check --proxy
Linkerd control plane linting:
 * can initialize the client ......................................[ok]
 * can query the Kubernetes API ..................................[ok]
Linkerd services health check:
 * control plane pods are running ................................[ok]
```

Such outputs from linkerd-check indicate the health and readiness of Linkerd components, ensuring all systems function as intended.

### Observability Enhancements

Prepare by implementing comprehensive logging, metrics, and tracing capabilities. Employ Prometheus and Grafana for metrics collection and visualization, ensuring that Linkerd's telemetry data provides actionable insights into service behavior.

Configure Linkerd to integrate seamlessly with distributed tracing tools like Jaeger or Zipkin to unravel the flow of requests across service boundaries, delivering visibility into latencies and bottlenecks.

```
linkerd install --set tracing.backend=jaeger | kubectl apply -f -
```

Ensure that logging levels are appropriately set to capture sufficient information without overwhelming storage resources.

### Policy and Governance Compliance

Align your deployment with organizational policies and any industry regulations like GDPR or HIPAA, especially concerning data handling. Validate compliance through regular audits, ensuring encryption protocols safeguard all data transiting through the service mesh.

Collaborate closely with compliance teams to understand any additional governance requirements that might necessitate custom configurations within Linkerd.

Each of these preparatory steps constitutes the backbone of a robust production deployment strategy for Linkerd. By addressing these areas proactively, teams can mitigate risks, optimize performance, and reinforce the security posture of their service meshes in production.

## 9.2 Managing Configuration and Secrets

In cloud-native applications and deployments, managing configuration settings and secrets securely and efficiently is a crucial component. Linkerd, being a service mesh that operates within Kubernetes, requires meticulous handling of configurations and secrets to ensure the security and reliability of microservices. This section delves into best practices and strategies for managing configurations and secrets associated with Linkerd in production environments, enabling organizations to maintain stringent security standards and operational efficiency.

**Understanding Configuration Options**

Linkerd configurations significantly influence the behavior of the service mesh in terms of routing policies, logging, and runtime adjustments. Centralizing configurations simplifies management and reduces the complexity associated with individual service configurations. Kubernetes provides several mechanisms for managing configurations, with ConfigMaps being prominent among them due to their flexibility and ease of use.

Using ConfigMaps allows teams to externalize configuration details from the containerized application image, promoting reuse and separation of concerns. For instance, a typical configuration might involve setting the logging level and configuring timeouts for Linkerd proxies:

```
apiVersion: v1
kind: ConfigMap
metadata:
  name: linkerd-config
  namespace: linkerd
data:
  proxy-log-level: debug
  inbound-idle-timeout: 30s
```

Mounting this ConfigMap into a Pod enables Linkerd to adopt these runtime configurations, enhancing the observability and responsiveness of the application.

**Secret Management Essentials**

Managing secrets such as API keys, TLS certificates, and tokens necessitates robust security mechanisms to prevent unauthorized access.

## 9.2. MANAGING CONFIGURATION AND SECRETS

Kubernetes offers built-in Secret objects to encapsulate sensitive data within the cluster securely. These secrets are base64 encoded and stored in etcd, which should be configured to encrypt data at rest for heightened security.

The syntax for a Kubernetes Secret might look like this:

```
apiVersion: v1
kind: Secret
metadata:
  name: linkerd-tls-cert
type: Opaque
data:
  tls.crt: <base64 encoded certificate>
  tls.key: <base64 encoded key>
```

For example, encrypting this data with etcd offers an additional layer of security:

```
--encryption-provider-config=/etc/kubernetes/encryption-config.yaml
```

### Integrating with External Secret Management Systems

Organizations often leverage external secret management solutions such as HashiCorp Vault, AWS Secrets Manager, or Azure Key Vault for advanced capabilities like automated secrets rotation and fine-grained access control. Integrating Linkerd with these systems can bolster security by centralizing sensitive information storage outside of Kubernetes, while still providing seamless access through synchronized configurations.

Configuring Linkerd to retrieve secrets from HashiCorp Vault, for example, involves the use of specific annotations in the workload manifest:

```
apiVersion: apps/v1
kind: Deployment
metadata:
  name: linkerd-deployment
  annotations:
    vault.hashicorp.com/agent-inject: "true"
    vault.hashicorp.com/agent-inject-secret-credentials: "secret/data/linkerd"
spec:
  template:
    metadata:
      annotations:
        vault.hashicorp.com/agent-inject: "true"
```

Such integrations ensure that secrets management remains scalable, secure, and compliant with organizational policies.

### Automating Configuration and Secret Updates

Automation streamlines the process of updating configurations and secrets, reducing the possibility of human error and the associated security risks. Employ CI/CD pipelines for automatic rolling updates of services when configurations or secrets change, thereby ensuring minimal service disruption.

Jenkins, GitLab CI, or GitHub Actions, in conjunction with Kubernetes' native tools, can facilitate this process. Use kubectl commands within a pipeline to apply new configurations:

```
kubectl apply -f linkerd-config.yaml
kubectl rollout restart deployment/linkerd
```

This approach enforces a revised deployment instantly reflecting configuration changes while adhering to best practices for zero-downtime updates.

### Implementing RBAC for Configuration and Secret Access

Role-Based Access Control (RBAC) is vital for limiting access to sensitive configurations and secrets to only those users who need it. Define clear roles and bind them to specific resources within the cluster to uphold the principle of least privilege.

Below is a sample configuration that binds an admin role to configmaps and secrets in the Linkerd namespace:

```
apiVersion: rbac.authorization.k8s.io/v1
kind: Role
metadata:
  namespace: linkerd
  name: config-secret-reader
rules:
- apiGroups: [""]
  resources: ["configmaps", "secrets"]
  verbs: ["get", "list", "watch"]
```

Combining RBAC with audit logs ensures adherence to policies while providing insights into access attempts and changes made.

### Mitigating Risks and Ensuring Auditability

The secure management of configurations and secrets extends beyond mere storage and retrieval. Establish audit logs to track access and

## 9.2. MANAGING CONFIGURATION AND SECRETS

modifications to these critical resources, enabling the rapid identification and rectification of suspicious activities or breaches.

Achieve full auditability by configuring Kubernetes audit policies to capture detailed logs:

```
apiVersion: audit.k8s.io/v1
kind: Policy
rules:
- level: Metadata
  resources:
  - group: ""
    resources: ["configmaps", "secrets"]
```

Such configuration logs every interaction with ConfigMaps and Secrets, serving as a comprehensive resource for forensic analysis.

### Best Practices and Policy Implementation

Adopt best practices and policies to fortify the management of configurations and secrets. Regularly rotate secrets, apply least privilege principles through RBAC, and maintain frequent backups of critical data. Alongside, employ tools such as OPA (Open Policy Agent) to ensure consistent policy enforcement across the cluster.

Implementing policies through OPA, for example, guarantees compliance and security adherence:

```
package kubernetes.admission
deny[msg] {
  input.request.kind.kind == "Secret"
  input.request.operation == "CREATE"
  input.request.object.data["tls.key"] != ""
  msg := "Secret creation denied unless properly encrypted"
}
```

This denies any attempt to create a Secret unless it adheres to specified security protocols, protecting sensitive data from being exposed inadvertently.

Effectively managing configurations and secrets in Linkerd deployments ensures not only the smooth operation of service meshes but also safeguards against security threats, enhancing the overall robustness and security resilience of cloud-native environments.

## 9.3 Ensuring High Availability

High availability (HA) is a critical requirement for production environments, particularly for service meshes like Linkerd, which play a central role in managing service-to-service communication. Ensuring high availability involves designing an infrastructure that remains operational and performant despite failures, maintenance activities, and varying loads. This section explores comprehensive strategies and techniques to ensure that Linkerd's deployment remains highly available, emphasizing redundancy, fault tolerance, and resilience.

**Architectural Redundancy**

Architectural redundancy is foundational to achieving high availability. In Kubernetes, this usually translates to deploying multiple replicas of Linkerd's control plane components across separate nodes or zones to ensure that no single point of failure exists. The critical components include the control plane pods, such as the controller, web, identity, and proxy injector. Deploying these components as StatefulSets or Deployments with more than one replica ensures availability even during node failures.

```
apiVersion: apps/v1
kind: Deployment
metadata:
  name: linkerd-controller
spec:
  replicas: 3
  selector:
    matchLabels:
      app: linkerd
  template:
    metadata:
      labels:
        app: linkerd
    spec:
      containers:
      - name: controller
        image: cr.l5d.io/linkerd/controller:stable
```

This setup configures three replicas of the 'linkerd-controller', thereby providing resilience against pod or node failures.

**Cross-Region and Multi-Zone Deployments**

For further resilience, consider deploying across multiple availability zones or even across geographic regions. This approach insulates

## 9.3. ENSURING HIGH AVAILABILITY

your deployment against regional outages, offering business continuity. Configuring Kubernetes clusters to operate in a multi-zone or multi-region setup requires the coordination of networking, persistent storage, and data replication strategies.

For example, use a Kubernetes cluster with node affinity and anti-affinity rules to ensure that replicas are distributed across zones:

```
apiVersion: apps/v1
kind: Deployment
metadata:
  name: linkerd-controller
spec:
  replicas: 3
  template:
    spec:
      affinity:
        podAntiAffinity:
          requiredDuringSchedulingIgnoredDuringExecution:
          - labelSelector:
              matchExpressions:
              - key: app
                operator: In
                values:
                - linkerd-controller
            topologyKey: "failure-domain.beta.kubernetes.io/zone"
```

Pod anti-affinity rules prevent multiple replicas from being scheduled on the same zone, thus enhancing fault tolerance.

### Load Balancing and Traffic Management

Effective load balancing and traffic management are key to distributing requests evenly and ensuring that no single component becomes overwhelmed. Linkerd uses Kubernetes' service-level load balancing to route traffic efficiently, while components like Ingress controllers or service meshes themselves can manage the traffic between services.

Deployment of an Ingress controller with Linkerd provides the gateway for directing external traffic appropriately:

```
apiVersion: networking.k8s.io/v1
kind: Ingress
metadata:
  name: linkerd-ingress
spec:
  rules:
  - host: linkerd.example.com
    http:
      paths:
      - path: /
        pathType: Prefix
```

```
          backend:
            service:
              name: linkerd-web
              port:
                number: 8084
```

The Ingress ensures that requests are balanced across the available replicas, optimizing resource use and throughput.

## Health Checks and Self-Healing

Automated health checks and self-healing mechanisms are critical for identifying failures and restoring service. Kubernetes natively offers liveness and readiness probes that can automatically restart failed pods or divert traffic away from unhealthy instances. Properly configured probes ensure the continued operation of Linkerd's components.

```
spec:
  containers:
  - name: controller
    livenessProbe:
      httpGet:
        path: /health
        port: 9990
      initialDelaySeconds: 30
      periodSeconds: 10
    readinessProbe:
      httpGet:
        path: /ready
        port: 9990
      initialDelaySeconds: 5
      periodSeconds: 10
```

Liveness probes trigger restarts of unresponsive pods, while readiness probes ensure traffic is only sent to healthy pods.

## Monitoring and Alerting Systems

Robust monitoring is crucial for maintaining high availability. Utilize Prometheus for fine-grained metric collection and Grafana for visualization, ensuring that all Linkerd components and the broader Kubernetes cluster are continuously observed. Alerts are configured to trigger notifications based on thresholds and anomalous patterns, enabling operators to respond promptly to issues.

Linkerd's integration with Prometheus offers endpoint monitoring:

```
scrape_configs:
  - job_name: 'linkerd'
    static_configs:
```

## 9.3. ENSURING HIGH AVAILABILITY

```
- targets: ['127.0.0.1:9990']
```

Accompanied by Grafana dashboards, these metrics provide actionable intelligence for maintaining HA setups.

### Disaster Recovery Planning

Effective disaster recovery (DR) strategies complement high availability arrangements. Regular backups of configuration states and data, along with defined RTO (Recovery Time Objective) and RPO (Recovery Point Objective), equip teams to recover from catastrophic failures without significant loss.

Use Velero for backup and restore functions in Kubernetes environments to ensure that recovery can be executed swiftly and predictably:

```
velero backup create linkerd-backup --include-namespaces=linkerd
```

Regularly test DR plans to confirm that procedures remain valid and that team members are prepared to execute them effectively.

### Rolling Updates and Blue-Green Deployments

Incorporating rolling updates and blue-green deployments minimizes downtime during upgrades or patch applications. Kubernetes supports these methodologies natively, allowing new replicas to be spun up and tested before the older version is shut down. This reduces service disruption, maintaining availability during transitions.

For example, use 'kubectl' for a progressive approach to updating replicas:

```
kubectl set image deployment/linkerd-controller controller=new-image:version
```

This command initiates a rolling update, providing a seamless transition between software versions.

Ensuring high availability within Linkerd deployments is a multifaceted endeavor involving architectural design, automation, and strategic planning. By applying these approaches diligently, organizations can foster environments capable of maintaining essential service operation amidst failures and demands, thereby safeguarding user experience and business continuity.

## 9.4 Continuous Integration and Deployment

Incorporating Continuous Integration (CI) and Continuous Deployment (CD) practices into the lifecycle of deploying Linkerd not only streamlines workflows but also enhances the reliability and consistency of service changes in production environments. This section explores the principles, advantages, and implementations of CI/CD pipelines tailored specifically for Linkerd deployments and the broader microservices architecture.

**Understanding CI/CD Principles**

At its core, CI/CD is about automating the integration and deployment process to ensure faster and more reliable software delivery. CI involves the automatic testing and merging of code changes to a central repository, while CD automates the deployment of validated code into production. This holistic approach simplifies the release process, reduces integration issues, and provides continuous feedback to development teams.

In the context of Linkerd, CI/CD processes can manage configurations, policies, and updates, ensuring the service mesh remains aligned with evolving service demands.

**Integrating Linkerd into CI Pipelines**

In a CI pipeline, the main goal is to integrate code changes as they occur. This requires the inclusion of automated testing, linting, and validation of both application code and Linkerd-specific configurations to identify issues early. Tools like Jenkins, CircleCI, TravisCI, and GitLab CI/CD are commonly used to create these pipelines.

For example, a simple CI setup using GitHub Actions might include the following workflow file:

```
name: CI Pipeline
on: [push]
jobs:
  build:
    runs-on: ubuntu-latest
    steps:
     - name: Checkout code
       uses: actions/checkout@v2
     - name: Set up Kubernetes
```

## 9.4. CONTINUOUS INTEGRATION AND DEPLOYMENT

```
    uses: azure/setup-kubectl@v1
    with:
      version: 'latest'
 - name: Run Linkerd Check
    run: |
      linkerd install | kubectl apply -f -
      linkerd check
 - name: Run Tests
    run: |
      go test -v ./...
```

This GitHub Actions pipeline automatically checks out the code, sets up Kubernetes, runs 'linkerd check' to validate the deployment, and executes unit tests, providing immediate feedback to developers.

**Ensuring Configuration and Policy Compliance**

Ensuring that Linkerd's configurations and policies are compliant with organizational guidelines is critical. Validation tools such as 'linkerd check' can be integrated as pre-deployment steps within the CI pipeline to verify the correctness and compatibility of configurations, preventing faulty deployments from progressing.

Utilizing 'kubectl' with additional linting tools also aids in maintaining compliance across the board:

```
kubectl apply --dry-run=client -f linkerd-config.yaml
kubeval linkerd-config.yaml
```

These commands simulate the application of configurations and validate them against Kubernetes' schema, catching potential errors early in the process.

**Automating Deployment with CD Pipelines**

CD focuses on the automated deployment of tested code to production, thus reducing manual intervention and expediting delivery cycles. With CD, once code has passed through the CI pipeline, it can be auto-deployed to different environments—development, staging, and ultimately production.

For example, GitLab CI/CD offers an integrated way to define complete CI/CD pipelines, facilitating seamless deployments:

```
stages:
  - test
  - deploy
```

```
test:
  stage: test
  script:
    - linkerd check
    - go test -v ./...

deploy:
  stage: deploy
  environment: production
  script:
    - kubectl apply -f linkerd-service.yaml
    - kubectl rollout status deployment/linkerd
  only:
    - main
```

In this pipeline, successful tests lead to immediate deployments of Linkerd services using 'kubectl', with rollout commands ensuring that the deployments are successful and stable.

**Blue-Green and Canary Deployments**

To further enhance deployment strategies, blue-green and canary deployments provide mechanisms to introduce new changes with reduced risk. Blue-green deployments maintain two identical environments—where one is active and the other idle. New changes deploy to the idle environment, and traffic switches only upon successful verification.

Canary deployments gradually route a small percentage of traffic to the new version before a full rollout, allowing time to monitor its impact on the system.

Linkerd's integration with such strategies involves modifying service configurations or leveraging traffic split features:

```
kubectl apply -f canary-service.yaml
linkerd install canary -f canary.yaml
kubectl patch svc/my-service -p '{"spec":{"selector":{"version":"canary"}}}'
```

Applying the 'canary-service.yaml' ensures only a subset of traffic is directed to the new version, minimizing risks while updating services.

**Using Helm for Configuration Management**

Helm charts come highly recommended for managing Linkerd configurations within CI/CD pipelines. They provide a templating mechanism for Kubernetes manifests, enabling dynamic setup and deployment across various environments.

## 9.4. CONTINUOUS INTEGRATION AND DEPLOYMENT

Define Helm values specific to each deployment stage:

```
replicas: 3
resources:
  limits:
    cpu: 200m
    memory: 512Mi
```

Packaging configurations as Helm charts provides flexibility, as settings can be parameterized and overridden using environment-specific values, preventing configuration drift.

### Ensuring Security and Authentication

In optimizing security within CI/CD workflows, ensure that all deployments authenticate changes, especially when dealing with sensitive configurations and secrets. Use Kubernetes Role-Based Access Control (RBAC) and secret management tools to ensure credentials are handled securely.

Integrate with secret management tools for fetching sensitive data during deployment:

```
vault kv get -field=value secret/linkerd | kubectl apply -f -
```

This integration ensures encrypted secrets remain outside version control yet are accessible in real-time during deployment processes.

### Monitoring and Rollback Protocols

Monitoring deployed services and having rollback mechanisms are necessary to maintain stability. Linkerd metrics should be actively monitored through systems like Prometheus, with alerts configured to notify any deviation from expected behaviors.

GitLab's built-in monitoring tools or third-party integrations create an observability layer for instant feedback:

```
prometheus:
  job_name: 'linkerd'
  metrics_path: '/metrics'
```

In emergency situations, rollbacks can be triggered manually or automatically through CI/CD pipelines, reducing mean time to recovery (MTTR) and ensuring that service degradation does not severely impact users.

The adoption of CI/CD practices with Linkerd leads to streamlined deployments, collaboration among teams, and accelerated delivery cycles. It creates a robust framework for managing microservices environments, ensuring that each update, once verified through continuous testing, is deployed reliably and securely. This not only reduces overheads but enables teams to focus on innovation, consistently delivering value to end-users.

## 9.5 Monitoring and Incident Response

In the operation of service meshes like Linkerd within production environments, monitoring and incident response become pivotal elements in maintaining system reliability and performance. This section provides an in-depth exploration of the strategies and tools utilized for effective monitoring and incident response, ensuring that any potential issues are swiftly identified, diagnosed, and resolved.

**The Importance of Monitoring**

Monitoring is the eyes and ears of a production environment, essential for understanding the health and performance of both Linkerd and the services it manages. Comprehensive monitoring not only ensures operational stability but also provides insights into user behavior and infrastructure utilization, enabling ongoing optimization.

Key monitoring metrics for Linkerd include latency, throughput, success rates, and error rates. These metrics give administrators visibility into the real-time performance of services and the ability to set thresholds for alerts.

**Leveraging Prometheus and Grafana**

Prometheus is a powerful open-source monitoring system widely used in Kubernetes environments for collecting metrics, while Grafana is employed for their visualization. Linkerd natively integrates with Prometheus to expose a wealth of metrics without requiring major configuration changes.

A Prometheus YAML configuration that scrapes Linkerd metrics might look like this:

```
scrape_configs:
```

## 9.5. MONITORING AND INCIDENT RESPONSE

```
- job_name: 'linkerd'
  metrics_path: '/metrics'
  kubernetes_sd_configs:
    - role: pod
  relabel_configs:
    - source_labels: [
        __meta_kubernetes_pod_label_linkerd_io_control_plane_component]
      action: keep
      regex: .+
```

This configuration targets Linkerd control plane pods and captures their metrics for further analysis.

Setting up Grafana to visualize these metrics involves installing Grafana dashboards specifically designed for Linkerd:

```
kubectl -n linkerd port-forward svc/grafana 3000:3000 &
# Access Grafana at http://localhost:3000, then import Linkerd dashboards
```

These dashboards offer a detailed view of system status, allowing operators to drill down into specific components to investigate issues.

### Defining Alerts and Notifications

Implementing alerting mechanisms in Prometheus ensures that potential issues are addressed swiftly before they escalate into incidents. Alerts are configured based on metric thresholds, such as elevated latency or reduced success rates over given periods.

Example alert configuration in Prometheus' alert rules:

```
groups:
- name: linkerd-alerts
  rules:
  - alert: LinkerdHighLatency
    expr: histogram_quantile(0.99, sum(rate(response_latency_ms_bucket[5m])) by (le
        )) > 500
    for: 10m
    labels:
      severity: critical
    annotations:
      summary: "Linkerd service latency is high"
      description: "Latency has exceeded 500ms for the past 10 minutes."
```

Prometheus can send these alerts to multiple notification channels such as PagerDuty, Slack, or email using Alertmanager.

### Diagnosis and Root Cause Analysis (RCA)

Upon receiving an alert, the incident response team must undertake a root cause analysis (RCA) to identify the source of issues. During this process, metrics stored in Prometheus, logs collected using a centralized logging solution like Elasticsearch, and traces obtained using distributed tracing tools like Jaeger can be invaluable.

Logs offer critical insights into system state changes. Set up Fluentd or a similar tool to aggregate logs across the Linkerd-managed environment for centralized access:

```
kubectl create -f fluentd-daemonset.yaml
# Fluentd will forward logs to Elasticsearch
```

Jaeger provides tracing capabilities, allowing teams to understand the transaction flow across services, pinpointing latency issues or failures:

```
kubectl create -f jaeger-all-in-one.yaml
# Instrument services with OpenTracing to start capturing tracing data
```

## Incident Response Processes

Developing a well-documented incident response plan is essential to restore service after an incident has been detected. The plan should include the following stages:

- Identification and Triage: Determine the severity of the incident using alerts and telemetry data.

- Communication: Inform stakeholders and affected users promptly.

- Containment: Mitigate immediate impacts by leveraging rollback capabilities or using traffic management strategies.

- Eradication: Identify and eliminate the root cause.

- Recovery: Restore affected services and verify system stability.

- Post-Incident Review: Conduct a detailed analysis to learn and improve future responses.

Ensure that all incident response actions are logged for accountability and later analysis.

## Review and Improvement Cycle

The conclusion of an incident should initiate a post-incident review or postmortem process. This involves gathering all logs, metrics, and traces related to the incident, as well as feedback from team members involved in the incident response. This information should be used to improve infrastructure resilience, refine alert thresholds, and optimize response procedures.

Regular review meetings fortify operational practices, allowing teams to:

- Update documentation and playbooks based on real incidents.
- Adjust monitoring setups to reduce false positives.
- Implement new automation to speed up future incident responses.

**Automated Response and Remediation**

Automated remediation actions can be embedded into incident response protocols to reduce human intervention time and mitigate impacts more swiftly. Utilize tools like Kubernetes Operators or AWS Lambda functions to perform predefined tasks automatically in response to specific alerts.

For example, an automated restart of high-latency pods might be triggered by a specific Prometheus alert:

```
kubectl patch deployment linkerd-controller -p '{"spec":{"replicas":1}}'
# Triggers a rolling restart of Linkerd pods in response to sustained alerts
```

By leveraging automation in this manner, teams can shorten the incident life cycle, enhancing service continuity.

By effectively integrating these monitoring and incident response mechanisms into Linkerd deployments, organizations can establish robust operations practices, ensuring that service interruptions are swiftly detected and addressed whilst maintaining service reliability and quality for end-users. This proactive approach not only safeguards system health but also empowers continuous improvement driven by operational insights.

## 9.6 Backup and Disaster Recovery

In the context of managing Linkerd-based service meshes in production environments, developing a robust backup and disaster recovery (BDR) strategy is essential for safeguarding against data loss and ensuring continuity in service operations. This section comprehensively explores the principles, strategies, and best practices involved in implementing effective BDR solutions tailored for environments that incorporate Linkerd within Kubernetes clusters.

**Understanding BDR Objectives**

The primary objectives of BDR involve minimizing downtime and data loss during catastrophic failures. Two critical metrics to define in BDR planning are:

- **Recovery Time Objective (RTO):** The maximum acceptable time to restore normal operations after a failure.

- **Recovery Point Objective (RPO):** The maximum tolerable period in which data might be lost due to a major incident.

These objectives guide the configuration of backup frequencies and the underlying architecture required to facilitate rapid recovery.

**Database Backups for Persistent Data**

For applications deployed on Kubernetes, databases often remain outside the ephemeral infrastructure hosted on persistent storage volumes. For backup, use industry-standard solutions like Velero for volume snapshots or SQL dumps for logical databases.

To back up persistent volume claims (PVCs) with Velero, follow this example:

```
velero backup create linkerd-db-backup --include-namespaces=linkerd --include-resources=persistentvolumeclaims
```

For databases like PostgreSQL, use `pg_dump` to perform logical backups:

```
PGPASSWORD=my_secure_password pg_dump -U postgres -h db.example.com -F c -b -v -f /backups/linkerd-pgsql-backup.dump linkerd
```

## 9.6. BACKUP AND DISASTER RECOVERY

Scheduling regular backups using cron jobs orchestrates this process, thereby aligning it with RPO targets.

### Configuration and Secret Backups

Configurations and secrets dictate the behavior and security of services. Kubernetes configures these through ConfigMaps and Secrets, which must be backed up to ensure services can be restored accurately. This can be automated through scripts or tools like Velero that support configuration snapshots.

Example Velero command for backing up ConfigMaps and Secrets:

```
velero backup create config-secret-backup --include-namespaces=linkerd --include-resources=configmaps,secrets
```

Ensure sensitive information is encrypted at rest, and safeguard access permissions when storing these backups.

### Cluster State Backups

Back up the Kubernetes cluster's state to capture its entire configuration. Use kubectl to export API resources and save them to a version control repository:

```
kubectl get all --all-namespaces -o yaml > cluster-state.yaml
```

Storing this YAML in a version control repository allows for tracking changes over time and quickly reverting to a known good state.

### Disaster Recovery Sites and Strategies

In addition to data protection, plan for infrastructure resilience by setting up disaster recovery sites. These provide failover capabilities to maintain operations in the event of a regional outage.

Two strategies include:

- **Active-Passive DR:** A secondary site sits idle until the primary site fails. Data replication is continuous, ensuring the secondary site is up-to-date for swift failover.

- **Active-Active DR:** Both sites actively handle traffic, offering immediate seamless failover capability. This demands sophisticated load balancing and synchronizing mechanisms.

Implementing geo-redundant infrastructure on cloud environments like AWS or GCP facilitates this aspect of disaster recovery.

**Data Replication Techniques**

Data replication is the linchpin for maintaining DR sites in sync. Techniques include:

- **Synchronous Replication:** Ensures data consistency between primary and secondary sites, albeit with more latency.

- **Asynchronous Replication:** Provides near real-time data updates with less impact on performance but risks minor data loss during abrupt failures.

Choose replication modes based on application criticality and RPO/RTO requirements.

Examples using storage-level replication tools:

```
aws s3 cp s3://source-bucket/data s3://replica-bucket/data --region us-west-2
```

**Automating Recovery Processes**

To meet defined RTO metrics, automate as much of the recovery process as possible. Utilize Infrastructure as Code (IaC) tools like Terraform or AWS CloudFormation to provision resources after a failure automatically.

Example of Infrastructure Codification for DR deployment:

```
Resources:
  MyInstance:
    Type: AWS::EC2::Instance
    Properties:
      InstanceType: t2.micro
      ImageId: ami-1234567890abcdef0
      KeyName: myKey
```

Automation scripts should include validation checks to ensure that the recovered state is working correctly before rerouting user traffic.

**Testing and Validation of BDR Plans**

Regular testing of backup and disaster recovery plans is crucial to ensure their effectiveness. Simulate disaster scenarios and perform recoveries to validate the timings, processes, and effectiveness of the strategy.

Run these validation scenarios quarterly, using defined KPIs to assess compliance with RTO/RPO objectives. Continuous improvement cycles based on test findings refine these strategies to increase reliability.

**Documentation and Training**

Comprehensive documentation is essential for any disaster recovery plan. It should include detailed instructions on the execution of recovery processes and the roles and responsibilities of involved personnel.

Conduct regular training sessions for team members to familiarize them with recovery steps, ensuring that everyone is prepared to respond swiftly and effectively during an actual incident.

By embedding these comprehensive backup and disaster recovery strategies within their Linkerd deployments, organizations can ensure resilience against data loss and service outages. Such measures not only protect organizational data and application availability but also build operational confidence, supporting ongoing business continuity in the face of unforeseen events.

# Chapter 10

# Future of Linkerd and Service Mesh Ecosystems

The evolution of service mesh technologies, including Linkerd, is pivotal for the future of cloud-native applications. This chapter explores upcoming trends and innovations that will shape service mesh ecosystems, such as increased integration with edge and serverless computing. It outlines the planned features and goals in Linkerd's future roadmap, emphasizing its role in multi-cloud environments. The chapter also examines the importance of Linkerd in supporting DevOps practices and site reliability engineering (SRE). Additionally, it highlights the significance of community contributions in driving advancements within the open-source ecosystem, signaling a collaborative path forward.

## 10.1 Evolving Trends in Service Mesh Technologies

The landscape of service mesh technologies has been evolving at an unprecedented pace, driven by the rapid development of cloud-native applications. This evolution is marked by several trends that are reshaping how service meshes are architected and deployed, significantly impacting their integration and management in cloud environments. This section delves into these evolving trends, examining key innovations, analyzing their implications, and illustrating how they contribute to the advancements in service mesh ecosystems.

Service mesh technologies, such as Linkerd, Istio, and Consul, have become critical components in managing the complex network of microservices that form cloud-native applications. These technologies provide a dedicated layer for managing service-to-service communication, offering features like traffic management, security, and observability. As organizations increasingly adopt microservices, the necessity for robust, easy-to-manage service meshes has prompted several innovative approaches and trends.

- Lightweight Architectures

    In recent years, there has been a shift towards more lightweight service mesh architectures, aiming to reduce the resource overhead traditionally associated with these technologies. Innovations such as Linkerd's adoption of Rust for performance-critical components exemplify this trend, allowing it to provide high efficiency without compromising on capabilities. The use of Rust enables lower memory footprints and reduced CPU utilization, facilitating its deployment in resource-constrained environments such as edge devices.

    ```
    # Example of a basic Linkerd service mesh installation
    curl -sL https://run.linkerd.io/install | sh
    linkerd install | kubectl apply -f -
    ```

    ```
    NAME      READY  STATUS
    linkerd   True   Linkerd is running
    ```

    This example demonstrates the simplicity of deploying a

lightweight Linkerd service mesh, showcasing its efficiency in both installation and execution.

- Zero-Trust Security Models

  The adoption of zero-trust security models within service mesh technologies is another prominent trend. This paradigm shift enhances security by implementing strict verification processes for each communication between services, regardless of their location in the network. The development of mutual TLS (mTLS) for encrypting service-to-service communications reflects this trend, providing automatic encryption without requiring application changes.

  ```
  const { createServer } = require('https');
  const fs = require('fs');

  const options = {
    key: fs.readFileSync('server-key.pem'),
    cert: fs.readFileSync('server-cert.pem'),
    ca: fs.readFileSync('cacert.pem'),
    requestCert: true,
    rejectUnauthorized: true,
  };

  createServer(options, (req, res) => {
    res.writeHead(200);
    res.end('hello, world!');
  }).listen(8000);
  ```

  This JavaScript snippet illustrates how mTLS can be implemented programmatically, ensuring that both server and client verify each other's identities.

- Enhanced Observability and Telemetry

  Improved observability and telemetry capabilities have become a cornerstone in service mesh development, emphasizing the need for detailed insights into service interactions and performance metrics. Advanced metrics collection and visualization provide crucial data that informs decision-making and optimizes performance. Service mesh projects are increasingly integrating with data visualization tools such as Prometheus and Grafana, allowing real-time monitoring and historical analysis.

  ```
  # Prometheus configuration for monitoring Linkerd
  scrape_configs:
    - job_name: 'linkerd'
  ```

```
  static_configs:
    - targets: ['localhost:9090']
```

```
# Grafana dashboard
- Panel ID: 1
- Graph Type: Line
- Metrics: Success Rate, Request Duration
```

The binding between Prometheus and Grafana facilitates comprehensive visibility into the service mesh, enabling teams to monitor metrics such as success rates and response times, vital for maintaining service health.

- Declarative Configuration and Automation

Service mesh technologies increasingly leverage declarative configuration models, which enhance automation and reduce human errors in managing configuration. Declarative tools such as Kubernetes Custom Resource Definitions (CRDs) have been instrumental in enabling self-healing and autoscaling features. This trend aligns with the broader movement towards Infrastructure-as-Code (IaC) practices, where configuration management is handled by code rather than manual processes.

```
# Example Kubernetes CRD for managing a Linkerd resource
apiVersion: linkerd.io/v1alpha1
kind: ServiceProfile
metadata:
  name: web-service.default.svc.cluster.local
spec:
  routes:
  - name: GET /reviews
    condition:
      method: GET
      path: /reviews
```

This YAML file defines a custom resource for Linkerd, specifying conditions to manage communication routes within the service mesh declaratively.

- Increased Focus on Multicluster and Hybrid Deployments

Multicluster and hybrid deployments represent another significant trend, responding to the needs of enterprises with diverse cloud strategies. Advances in service mesh technologies are enabling seamless management of services across multiple environments, whether on-premises, in public clouds, or across different

## 10.1. EVOLVING TRENDS IN SERVICE MESH TECHNOLOGIES

cloud providers. This capability allows organizations to leverage the benefits of a multi-cloud architecture, such as increased resilience and reduced vendor lock-in.

```
# Example command to enable multicluster support in Linkerd
linkerd multicluster install | kubectl apply -f -
```

```
multicluster status: enabled
multicluster gateways: ready
```

The command above illustrates the ease with which Linkerd can be adapted to support multicluster configurations, facilitating communication between disparate environments.

- Integration with Emerging Technologies

  Service meshes are increasingly integrating with emerging technologies such as edge computing and serverless architectures. This integration is crucial for applications that demand low-latency communication and deployment flexibility. The ability to deploy services closer to the end-users using edge nodes, while maintaining a cohesive service mesh, expands the potential use cases and enhances performance.

  Integration with serverless platforms allows service meshes to extend their features to serverless functions, ensuring they can participate in service-to-service operations with the same security and observability benefits applied to traditional services.

```
# Command to deploy edge-optimized Linkerd
linkerd edge install | kubectl apply -f -
```

```
edge deployment: initialized
status: operational
```

By deploying an edge-optimized version of Linkerd, organizations can improve the performance of latency-sensitive applications.

- Enhanced Support for DevOps and SRE Practices

  Service mesh technologies are aligning increasingly with DevOps and Site Reliability Engineering (SRE) practices. Automated pipelines, blue-green deployments, and canary releases are just some of the strategies now supported more seamlessly by service meshes. These features promote a culture of rapid iteration, experimentation, and resilience, which are central to modern software development practices.

```
# Python script example using Flagger for canary release
import flagger

flagger.deploy_canary('web-service')
flagger.promote('web-service', 'latest')
```

This Python script showcases using Flagger to manage canary deployments, providing an automated mechanism to roll out changes gradually and monitor their impact.

- Standardization and Interoperability Efforts

  Standardization and interoperability play an essential role in the evolution of service mesh technologies. Efforts such as the Service Mesh Interface (SMI) are aimed at providing a set of standardized APIs that service meshes can implement, enhancing compatibility and ease of use. This enables tools and applications to work seamlessly across different service mesh implementations, fostering a diverse ecosystem.

```
# SMI Traffic Split Example
apiVersion: split.smi-spec.io/v1alpha2
kind: TrafficSplit
metadata:
  name: service-split
spec:
  service: web-service
  backends:
  - service: web-service-v1
    weight: 80
  - service: web-service-v2
    weight: 20
```

This example showcases the use of the SMI specification to implement traffic splitting, directing traffic between multiple versions of a service based on predefined weights.

As service mesh technologies continue to evolve, these trends highlight their expanding capabilities and integration with broader cloud-native ecosystems. Each innovation not only addresses current challenges but also sets the stage for new opportunities in building scalable, efficient, and robust microservices architectures. These evolving trends in service mesh technologies underscore the dynamic, rapidly advancing nature of the field, providing critical infrastructure aligned with future-facing application development.

## 10.2 Future Roadmap for Linkerd

The Future Roadmap for Linkerd outlines the development path, anticipated features, and strategic goals that are poised to drive its progressive enhancements. This section provides a comprehensive exploration of these elements, emphasizing the alignment with community-driven goals and emerging technological trends. The roadmap not only illuminates Linkerd's evolution but also offers insight into how it intends to maintain and expand its role within the broader service mesh and cloud-native landscapes.

Linkerd, recognized for its simplicity and reliability, continues to evolve by responding to both the dynamic demands of modern applications and the feedback from its vibrant user community. The following points detail the significant areas of focus and anticipated developments that constitute Linkerd's future roadmap.

- Performance Optimization and Scaling

    A key objective for Linkerd is to enhance its performance scalability. As service meshes continue to manage an increasing number of services due to the proliferation of microservices architectures, ensuring minimal latency and efficient resource use becomes critical. Linkerd is committed to refining its Rust-based components, optimizing execution paths, and reducing overhead to enable deployment in environments with stringent resource constraints, such as edge computing.

    ```
    # Command to bench test Linkerd's performance
    linkerd bench --num-replicas=50 --concurrency=8
    ```

    Performance results:
    Latency (p50): 5ms
    Throughput: 1000 requests/sec

This illustrative command and output demonstrate how Linkerd's performance can be quantitatively assessed and optimized through benchmarking.

- Advanced Traffic Management Features

On the roadmap are advanced traffic management capabilities designed to provide refined control over service communication. These include more sophisticated routing rules, traffic mirroring, and adaptive load balancing interventions based on real-time traffic conditions. By integrating with machine learning models, Linkerd can leverage predictive analytics to anticipate traffic spikes and adaptively redistribute loads.

```yaml
# YAML configuration for traffic mirroring in Linkerd
apiVersion: linkerd.io/v1alpha1
kind: TrafficSplit
metadata:
  name: example-split
spec:
  service: backend
  backends:
  - service: backend-v1
    weight: 80
  - service: backend-v2
    weight: 20
  - service: mirror-backend
    mirror: true
```

This configuration illustrates a traffic mirroring setup, which duplicates live traffic to a secondary service for testing new features under production-like conditions.

- Security Enhancements

Security stands as a pivotal element in Linkerd's roadmap, with ongoing developments focusing on extending its zero-trust model and fortifying its cryptographic frameworks. Enhancements are expected in areas such as automatic key rotation, integration with external authentication and authorization services, and fine-grained access control. Linkerd aims to simplify compliance with regulatory standards, offering built-in reporting and audit capabilities regarding data privacy and service interaction history.

```
Certificates will rotate automatically every 24 hours.
Enhanced security plugins for external IAM integration planned.
```

## 10.2. FUTURE ROADMAP FOR LINKERD

This brief note highlights intended improvements in security protocols and integrations, ensuring Linkerd meets evolving security demands.

- Improved Observability and Debugging Tools

With a focus on observability, Linkerd's roadmap includes the introduction of enhanced tracing and debugging tools. These tools facilitate deeper insight into the service mesh's operations, helping to swiftly resolve outages and performance bottlenecks. New features will include enhanced logging facilities, support for tracing standards like OpenTelemetry, and improved visualization capabilities integrated directly within the Linkerd dashboard.

```
# Command to enable tracing in Linkerd
linkerd tap --namespace=default
```

```
Tracing enabled: true
Collected trace count: 1500 traces/minute
```

Executing the command above enables tracing, illustrating Linkerd's potential in comprehensively monitoring requests across services.

- User Experience and Interface Enhancements

User experience remains a cornerstone in Linkerd's roadmap with plans to streamline the user interface further and simplify configuration processes. Providing intuitive dashboards regardless of complexity in the service architecture is a priority. Enhancements will include more responsive designs, customization options for dashboards, and interactive tutorials guiding new users through setup and configuration, ensuring Linkerd maintains its reputation for accessibility and ease of use.

> Upcoming UI features include drag-and-drop dashboard widgets and real-time updates.

Anticipated user interface enhancements offer users more personalized and dynamic interaction, contributing significantly to Linkerd's user friendliness.

- Integration with Emerging Cloud-Native Technologies

Linkerd positions itself to integrate with contemporary cloud-native technologies and paradigms, such as serverless computing and Kubernetes Operators. Planned developments include support for proxyless gRPC services and enhanced compatibility with serverless frameworks, allowing Linkerd to provide robust service management across various cloud-native architectures seamlessly.

```
# Enabling serverless compatibility in Linkerd
linkerd serverless install | kubectl apply -f -
```

Serverless support: active
Compatible runtimes: AWS Lambda, Azure Functions, Google Cloud Functions

The command exemplifies how Linkerd enhances its cloud-native integration capabilities, facilitating more diverse application architectures.

- Community Engagement and Open Source Contributions

In accordance with its open-source ethos, Linkerd's roadmap is heavily influenced by community interactions and contributions. Strategic initiatives include increasing support for contributors through better documentation, establishing more direct lines of communication between users and maintainers, and organizing community events aimed at knowledge sharing and collaboration. Encouraging community-driven feature requests ensures Linkerd continues to address real-world use cases and remains aligned with users' needs.

```
Community workshops and hackathons planned for next year.
Contributors receive priority access to support channels.
```

These engagements not only foster innovation but also solidify Linkerd's position as a leading community-driven service mesh project.

- Strategic Alliances and Collaborations

Future endeavors will also explore strategic alliances with technology leaders to enhance Linkerd's capabilities and reach. Partnerships with providers of telemetry, security, and analytics solutions will pave the way for bundled offerings that simplify deployment and management for enterprises. Collaborative efforts aim to build a more interconnected ecosystem where Linkerd can leverage external tools to expand its baseline functionality without increasing complexity.

> Potential collaborations with Grafana for embedded analytics and Datadog for integrated monitoring.

These strategic partnerships will extend Linkerd's operational capabilities, offering users more cohesive and integrated solutions.

The Linkerd roadmap is not only a reflection of anticipated technical milestones but an embodiment of its commitment to advancing the state of the art in service mesh technologies. The outlined strategic goals align with the needs of modern enterprises, ensuring Linkerd remains pivotal in enhancing cloud-native operational excellence. Through a combination of technological advancements and community-driven initiatives, Linkerd is set to maintain its influential role in the evolution of service mesh ecosystems, continually adapting to the changing landscape of software architecture.

## 10.3 Integration with Emerging Technologies

As service mesh technologies continue to gain prominence within cloud-native architectures, their integration with emerging technologies becomes increasingly vital. This section details how Linkerd, a leading service mesh platform, is strategically positioning itself to collaborate with and support next-generation technologies such as edge computing, serverless architectures, and artificial intelligence/machine learning. Through innovative integration strategies, Linkerd aims to enhance operational efficiencies, performance, and adaptability in a dynamically evolving technological environment.

The seamless integration of service meshes like Linkerd with emerging technologies is crucial for organizations aiming to leverage these advancements to optimize performance and resource utilization. Discussing these integrations offers insights into how Linkerd enhances its core capabilities to adapt to and interact with these technological trends.

- Edge Computing

  Edge computing extends computational capabilities closer to the source of data generation, often at or near IoT devices or sensors, to reduce latency and bandwidth use. Linkerd is ideally suited to support edge computing scenarios due to its lightweight proxy architecture and focus on minimal resource overhead. Ensuring encrypted and efficient service communication at the edge necessitates optimizing Linkerd for constrained environments where CPU and memory are limited.

  ```
  # Command to deploy Linkerd in an edge environment
  linkerd install --ha --controller-replicas=3 | kubectl apply -f -
  ```

  Linkerd deployed with high availability settings optimized for edge nodes.

  The provided command illustrates deploying Linkerd in a high-availability configuration tailored for edge computing environments, ensuring robust and optimized service communication.

- Serverless Architectures

  As serverless computing models, such as those offered by AWS Lambda, Google Cloud Functions, and Azure Functions, continue to rise, Linkerd is advancing its efforts to integrate service mesh functionality with serverless workflows. Traditionally, serverless architectures abstract server management, allowing developers to focus solely on code, but often lack built-in mechanisms for consistent service communication and monitoring across functions. Linkerd aims to fill this gap by providing observability, security, and control beyond traditional service architectures.

  ```
  # Command to set up Linkerd with serverless functions
  linkerd serverless connect --provider=aws_lambda --region=us-east-1
  ```

  Linkerd serverless connection established with AWS Lambda in us-east-1 region.

  This command configures Linkerd to manage serverless functions, exemplifying how service mesh responsibilities can extend into serverless environments, providing unified controls.

## 10.3. INTEGRATION WITH EMERGING TECHNOLOGIES

- Artificial Intelligence and Machine Learning

  Integrating with AI and ML platforms represents another frontier for Linkerd, enabling intelligent decision-making processes and adaptive management systems. Service meshes can enhance AI workflows by providing data integrity, latency optimization, and secure data transit between AI components. Linkerd's observability features can be leveraged to monitor AI model interactions, resource utilization, and performance metrics, critical for tuning and scaling AI solutions.

  ```
  # Python script example for integrating with an ML pipeline
  import linkerd
  import tensorflow as tf

  # Monitor model inference requests
  linkerd.observe('model-inference').start()

  # ML model setup
  model = tf.keras.models.load_model('saved_model/my_model')

  # Inference function
  def predict(input_data):
      linkerd.log_request(input_data)
      prediction = model.predict(input_data)
      linkerd.log_response(prediction)
      return prediction
  ```

  This Python script demonstrates the integration between Linkerd and a machine learning pipeline, showcasing how it can aid in monitoring and logging model requests and predictions.

- Blockchain Technologies

  Blockchain integration with service mesh technologies like Linkerd can enhance secure and verifiable transaction processes. By ensuring integrity and observability throughout blockchain operations, Linkerd facilitates decentralized applications (dApps) needing consistent and resilient network communication. Through its robust security features, Linkerd can assist in maintaining traceability and authenticity of data exchanges inherent to blockchain processes.

  ```
  /* JavaScript example for a dApp using Linkerd */
  const Web3 = require('web3');
  const linkerd = require('linkerd');

  // Set up blockchain client
  ```

```
const web3 = new Web3(new Web3.providers.HttpProvider("http://localhost
    :8545"));

// Contract interaction with enhanced Linkerd logging
async function logTransaction(transaction) {
    linkerd.log_transaction(transaction.hash);
    await web3.eth.sendTransaction(transaction);
    linkerd.log_transaction_success(transaction.hash);
}
```

This code snippet highlights how Linkerd can help log and monitor blockchain transactions, ensuring reliable and secure application behavior within decentralized environments.

- Internet of Things (IoT)

    IoT integration places unique demands on service meshes due to the sheer number of connected devices and the need for efficient communication. Linkerd's lightweight design and ability to operate in constrained environments enable it to manage IoT networks effectively. By optimizing latency, enhancing security, and providing visibility into IoT traffic patterns, Linkerd can improve the performance and reliability of IoT deployments.

```
# Script to install Linkerd with IoT devices
linkerd install --iot --proxy-init-image=linkerd/proxy-init:stable | kubectl apply -
    f -
```

IoT deployment initialized, Linkerd proxy setup completed for IoT traffic routing.

The command demonstrates deploying Linkerd within IoT settings, optimizing its operation for network topologies frequently encountered with IoT devices.

- Multi-cloud Strategies

    Organizations embracing multi-cloud strategies require tools capable of managing service mesh extensions across various clouds, ensuring seamless service communication and management. Linkerd's capability in multi-cluster environments extends to supporting multi-cloud deployments, offering reliability, security, and observability without cloud vendor restrictions, allowing organizations to maximize flexibility and avoid lock-in.

## 10.3. INTEGRATION WITH EMERGING TECHNOLOGIES

```
# Example command to manage multi-cloud integration
linkerd multicluster connect --context=gke_cluster --region=us-west1
```

Multi-cloud connection established with GKE cluster in us-west1 region.

This command enables Linkerd to manage services over multiple cloud providers, reinforcing its adaptability across complex cloud environments.

- Data Analytics and Big Data

  Data analytics platforms increasingly utilize service meshes to secure and streamline data pipelines. Linkerd facilitates the management of distributed data processing tasks, ensuring secure, efficient data transit across clusters. Its integration aids in real-time analytics, reducing bottlenecks and optimizing data flow dependencies crucial for big data operations.

```java
// Java snippet for integrating Linkerd with an Apache Spark job
import org.apache.spark.SparkConf;
import org.apache.spark.api.java.JavaSparkContext;
import linkerd.SparkLinkerd;

// Configure Spark job with Linkerd
SparkConf conf = new SparkConf().setAppName("LinkerdIntegrationExample")
;
conf.set("spark.executor.instances", "5");
JavaSparkContext sparkContext = new JavaSparkContext(conf);

SparkLinkerd linkerd = new SparkLinkerd(sparkContext);
linkerd.enableObservability();

// Proceed with data processing
```

This Java example showcases integrating Linkerd with Apache Spark to inform and optimize data processing workflows in big data analytics.

- High-Performance Computing (HPC)

  Linkerd's integration with HPC environments provides enhanced manageability and security of workloads that demand significant computational power. By ensuring reliable, low-latency communication between distributed HPC resources, Linkerd contributes to the efficiency and speed of computational processes. This integration aids in managing network services in scientific computation, simulations, or rendering tasks.

```
# HPC Grid Linkerd configuration - optimized for high throughput and low
    latency
proxy:
  resources:
    requests:
      cpu: 200m
      memory: 512Mi
    limits:
      cpu: 1
      memory: 1Gi
```

This configuration snippet clarifies how Linkerd is optimized for efficient task execution in HPC environments, maintaining critical performance characteristics across compute nodes.

Linkerd's strategic efforts to integrate with emerging technologies aim to expand its utility and relevance within a rapidly changing technical landscape. By evolving alongside these innovations, Linkerd is enhancing its value proposition as a service mesh platform capable of supporting diverse and cutting-edge use cases. Through thoughtful integration, Linkerd not only fortifies its core offerings but also positions itself at the forefront of technological advancement, providing synergistic value across prevalent technological paradigms.

## 10.4 Multi-Cloud Strategies for Linkerd

- Environmental Compliance

    Linkerd can be configured to comply with various environmental regulations. For instance, the following configuration ensures that data handling adheres to GDPR:

```
eu-central
  compliance: GDPR
```

    This policy illustrates how Linkerd can be used to direct traffic in compliance with data residency laws, ensuring data remains within specified regions.

- Disaster Recovery and High Availability

    Multi-cloud strategies can bolster disaster recovery efforts by providing redundant infrastructures across diverse geographical and provider landscapes. Linkerd's service mesh capabilities support high availability by enabling seamless failover and redundancy strategies across cloud environments, ensuring service continuity in the face of provider-specific outages.

```
# Script to configure Linkerd for high availability across clouds
linkerd multicluster link --context=primary_aks --backup-context=secondary_eks
linkerd install --ha --context=primary_aks | kubectl apply -f -
```

High availability configuration active.
Primary AKS and backup EKS clusters linked for disaster recovery.

Deploying Linkerd with high availability settings ensures that services can gracefully degrade and failover, preserving uptime and reliability.

- Environment-Specific Optimization

Linkerd's design facilitates optimization for specific environments by enabling resource constraints to be tailored per cloud service, effectively utilizing the varied resource offerings of each provider. Through context-specific configurations that adjust resource limits, Linkerd aligns seamlessly with the resource management strategies of different clouds.

```
# Example of cloud-specific resource optimization
context: aws_cluster
  linkerd:
    proxy:
      resources:
        requests:
          cpu: 250m
          memory: 512Mi
context: gcp_cluster
  linkerd:
    proxy:
      resources:
        requests:
          cpu: 300m
          memory: 1Gi
```

This multi-context configuration shows how Linkerd can be optimized for various cloud settings, accommodating different pricing models and performance capabilities.

- Collaboration with Cloud Vendors

Linkerd's commitment to multi-cloud adaptability also involves collaboration with major cloud providers to improve integration layers and take advantage of specific cloud capabilities. Strategic partnerships facilitate smoother operations and optimize Linkerd's functionality to utilize proprietary services like AWS PrivateLink or Azure ExpressRoute.

```
# Note on collaborative efforts with cloud providers
Upcoming integrations with AWS Transit Gateway
Advanced support for Azure's Virtual Network Peering
```

These cooperative efforts with cloud vendors allow Linkerd to take full advantage of infrastructure capabilities, enhancing multi-cloud architectures' flexibility and efficiency.

- Seamless Development and Deployment Pipelines

Linkerd supports the development and deployment amplifications necessary for multi-cloud systems by integrating with CI/CD pipelines. This aid provision automates deployments across cloud platforms, ensuring consistent rollout practices and reducing time-to-market for application features and updates.

```
# Python CI/CD pipeline integration example
from kubernetes import client, config
import linkerd

config.load_kube_config()
v1 = client.CoreV1Api()

def deploy_linkerd(version):
    linkerd.install(version=version, context="aws_cluster")
    linkerd.install(version=version, context="gcp_cluster")
    print(f"Deployed Linkerd version {version} to all clusters.")

# Run deployment
deploy_linkerd("stable-2.12.3")
```

This Python script demonstrates a deployment pipeline integration with Linkerd, highlighting automation capabilities for multi-cloud environments.

By adapting to multi-cloud environments, Linkerd significantly enhances the potential for organizations to optimize resilience, security, and efficiency in their microservice deployments. Addressing challenges inherent to distributed cloud architectures, Linkerd provides a service mesh that is robust, adaptable, and secure, making it an indispensable asset in modern multi-cloud strategies. Its continued development ensures it remains ahead of the curve, accommodating the evolving needs of enterprises leveraging heterogeneous cloud services. Through a dedicated focus on seamless integration, comprehensive observability, and optimal policy enforcement, Linkerd empowers organizations to fully realize the benefits of a multi-cloud approach.

## 10.5 Role of Linkerd in DevOps and SRE

Linkerd plays a pivotal role in the modern landscapes of DevOps and Site Reliability Engineering (SRE) by providing a comprehensive toolkit for managing the complexities of microservices architectures. This section delves into the ways Linkerd supports continuous integration and delivery processes, enables automation, enhances system reliability, and facilitates efficient incident response. These capabilities make it an indispensable component in accelerating DevOps workflows and reinforcing the principles of SRE, which emphasize maintaining and improving system reliability and operational capacity amidst continuous change.

DevOps and SRE are two critical paradigms in contemporary software development and IT operations, prioritizing rapid delivery cycles, system resilience, and continuous improvement. Linkerd supports both through its service mesh capability, offering tools and features that streamline processes and bolster system robustness.

- Automating Service Management

    Linkerd facilitates the automation of service management tasks, aligning tightly with DevOps practices centered on incorporating automation to foster efficiency and reduce manual intervention. By automating aspects such as traffic routing, mTLS certificates, and service dependencies, Linkerd significantly reduces the complexities associated with managing microservices.

    ```
    # Script to automate Linkerd mTLS configuration
    linkerd install --tls=optional --ha | kubectl apply -f -
    linkerd check --tls
    ```

# CHAPTER 10. FUTURE OF LINKERD AND SERVICE MESH ECOSYSTEMS

```
TLS configuration validated successfully.
Automated mTLS setup complete.
```

Automating the installation and configuration of mTLS ensures security practices are consistently applied across all services without direct manual configurations.

- Enhancing Observability

The observability function in Linkerd is a cornerstone for both DevOps and SRE. By providing real-time telemetry, metrics, and service behavior insights, Linkerd empowers teams to understand application performance deeply and identify areas for enhancement. This observational capability supports SRE's mandate to maintain effective monitoring and alerting practices, ensuring system health and reliability.

```
# Command to view metrics and logs for enhanced observability
linkerd viz metrics
linkerd viz logs --namespace=production
```

```
CPU Usage: 45%
Memory Usage: 60%
Error Rate: 0.5%
```

This example demonstrates how service metrics can be accessed to inform capacity planning, incident mitigation, and performance optimization efforts.

- Seamless Continuous Integration and Deployment (CI/CD) Pipelines

Linkerd integrates seamlessly into CI/CD workflows, a fundamental aspect of DevOps practices. By providing consistent deployment environments and facilitating feature isolation through canary releases and blue-green deployments, Linkerd helps teams maintain software stability amid frequent deployment cycles.

```
// Jenkins Pipeline configuration for deploying services with Linkerd
pipeline {
    agent any
    stages {
        stage('Build') {
            steps {
```

## 10.5. ROLE OF LINKERD IN DEVOPS AND SRE

```
            sh 'mvn clean package'
        }
    }
    stage('Deploy to Staging') {
        steps {
            sh 'kubectl apply -f k8s/staging.yaml'
            sh 'linkerd inject k8s/staging.yaml | kubectl apply -f -'
        }
    }
    stage('Canary Release') {
        steps {
            sh 'linkerd rollcanary update --context=prod_cluster'
        }
    }
}
post {
    always {
        sh 'linkerd viz stat'
    }
}
}
```

The Jenkins pipeline script illustrates the integration of Linkerd into a build and deployment process, demonstrating how it supports stage isolation and implementation of canary releases for risk mitigation.

- Supporting Reliable Operations

  Reliability forms the core of SRE practices, where maintaining system uptime and minimizing disruptions are paramount. Linkerd supports these goals by providing automatic failover, load balancing, and traffic shaping capabilities, ensuring system robustness against failures.

```
# Configuration for automatic failover in Linkerd
apiVersion: linkerd.io/v1alpha1
kind: Failover
metadata:
  name: service-failover
spec:
  source: primary-service
  target: backup-service
```

This configuration establishes automatic fallback routes in case of service failure, enabling continuity and delivering a higher level of reliability.

- Facilitating Incident Response and Postmortems

  Linkerd enhances the speed and accuracy of incident response, aligning with SRE's focus on reducing mean time to recovery (MTTR). Through comprehensive logging and trace capabilities, Linkerd allows teams to quickly ascertain the root cause of performance issues or service interruptions, leading to faster remediation.

```
# Command to trace service requests for incident diagnosis
linkerd tap deploy/backend --to svc/frontend --namespace=production
```

| Timestamp | Source | Destination |
|---|---|---|
| 07:21:03 | 10.0.0.12 | 10.0.0.42 |

In the event of an incident, detailed request tracing helps teams identify bottlenecks or faults in the service chain, which is crucial for rapid recovery and iterative improvements.

- Enforcing Consistent Security Policies

Security remains a foundational concern in DevOps and SRE implementations. Linkerd enforces consistent security policies across microservices, utilizing mTLS for encryption and authentication, thus maintaining a security-first approach that aligns with SRE's objectives for reliable and safe operations.

```
# Security context to enforce identity validation
context:
  principal: secure-user
  linkerd:
    authorize:
      strict: true
```

This security context ensures all requests and interactions between services are authenticated, maintaining the integrity of the system while reducing potential security vulnerabilities.

- Load Testing and Performance Benchmarking

DevOps practices integrate continuous performance assessment to ensure software delivers expected levels amid evolving demands. Linkerd's load testing and benchmarking capabilities equip engineers with the tools to simulate traffic, stress test systems, and uncover potential scalability issues.

```
# Simple script for load testing a Linkerd service
kubectl run -it --rm load-generator --image=busybox /bin/sh
loadtest() {
```

## 10.5. ROLE OF LINKERD IN DEVOPS AND SRE

```
for i in {1..1000}; do
  wget -O- http://primary-service:8080 > /dev/null
done
}
loadtest
```

Running such a script automates service load generation, providing meaningful insights into how application stack performance varies under different workload conditions.

- Promoting a Culture of Collaboration

The implementation of Linkerd in DevOps and SRE not only serves technical uses but encourages cultural shifts toward collaborative efforts between development and operations teams. Linkerd's straightforward setup and API clarity enhance communication across teams by providing a common understanding of service behavior and expectations.

```
# Example of collaborative configuration documentation
Team A - responsible for frontend services:
  - Ensure Linkerd annotations are up-to-date for all frontend deployments.
Team B - manages backend services:
  - Monitor Linkerd observability dashboards to ensure backend efficiency.
```

Collaboratively maintained documentation enhances transparency and cooperative troubleshooting, leading to better alignment and shared goals.

- Agile Incident Management

Adopting agile methodologies for incident management requires dynamic strategies to navigate unplanned service degradations with nimbleness. Linkerd's features contribute to agile responsiveness by facilitating traffic diversion techniques and adaptive scalability alignments.

```
# Declarative configuration for agile traffic rerouting
apiVersion: traffic.linkerd.io/v1alpha1
kind: TrafficShift
metadata:
  name: dynamic-reroute
spec:
  source: app-service
  condition:
    latencyThreshold: 200ms
  target:
    - fallback-service
```

Traffic can be rerouted dynamically based on real-time conditions, ensuring minimal impact on user experience and maintaining high service levels.

Linkerd's deep integration into the DevOps and SRE domains showcases its versatile capabilities in reinforcing operational transparency, delivering robust service resilience, and ensuring a high-quality software delivery lifecycle. By bridging technical innovation and cultural integration, Linkerd empowers teams to navigate the complexities of modern microservices-centric ecosystems effectively. Its focus on automation, observability, and security provides a cohesive framework supporting both developmental agility and operational stability, fulfilling critical DevOps and SRE responsibilities in maintaining software integrity, performance, and reliability.

## 10.6 Community and Open Source Contributions

The role of community and open source contributions in the development and evolution of Linkerd is both foundational and transformative. This section explores how community engagement drives innovation, fosters collaboration, and enhances the resilience of Linkerd's development ecosystem. It examines the structures in place for community participation and the impact of collaborative development on Linkerd's features and stability. Additionally, it highlights the importance of open source principles in cultivating a shared sense of ownership and responsibility among diverse contributors globally.

Community and open source development are central tenets of Linkerd's success, providing a platform for collaboration that transcends geographic and organizational boundaries. This open, participatory model not only accelerates development cycles but ensures that Linkerd remains attuned to the actual needs and challenges faced by its user base.

- Community-Driven Innovation

    The vitality of Linkerd's development is deeply rooted in its active

## 10.6. COMMUNITY AND OPEN SOURCE CONTRIBUTIONS

and engaged community. Contributors from varied backgrounds – ranging from individual hobbyists to enterprise users – bring unique perspectives and skills that fuel innovation across the project. New features and improvements often originate from community suggestions and pull requests, reflecting real-world user requirements and operational contexts.

```
# Example of a community-driven feature proposal
Feature: Dynamic mTLS Certificate Rotation
Description: Automatically rotate service certificates every 24 hours to enhance
    security without causing downtime.
Contributor: user123
```

This feature proposal showcases a typical community initiative where discussions around security and automation inspired development ideas, later implemented by the project maintainers.

- Collaborative Development Workflow

  Linkerd's development follows a collaborative workflow that empowers contributors to participate actively in new feature development, bug fixes, and documentation enhancements. Community members engage through GitHub, where issues are discussed openly, allowing for transparent problem-solving processes and maintaining a shared repository of knowledge.

```
# Git command example for community contributions
git clone https://github.com/linkerd/linkerd2.git
git checkout -b feature/new-metrics-collection
# Implement new feature
git commit -am "Added new metrics collection feature"
git push origin feature/new-metrics-collection
```

This Git process illustrates how contributors set up their feature branches, develop new capabilities, and actively participate in Linkerd's development life cycle, enhancing both the platform and their skills.

- Open Source Governance and Structure

  Linkerd's governance model is structured to facilitate open decision-making processes, ensuring that strategic direction aligns with the community and stakeholder interests. Governance includes a steering committee of seasoned contributors who guide the project's long-term vision while creating space for new voices to influence software progression.

## CHAPTER 10. FUTURE OF LINKERD AND SERVICE MESH ECOSYSTEMS

```
# Example extract from governance document
Steering Committee Roles:
- Set project priorities and feature roadmaps
- Facilitate community engagement and meetups
- Ensure alignment with CNCF goals
Contributors' Workshop:
- Quarterly meetings to gather feedback and set goals
```

This segment of the governance documentation provides insight into how roles are structured and responsibilities are distributed, safeguarding the project's open governance ethos.

- Fostering Inclusivity and Diversity

A key triumph for Linkerd is its broad inclusivity, encouraging participation from a wide array of contributors regardless of region, company affiliation, or experience level. Initiatives such as mentorship programs, inclusive documentation, and community meetups aim to lower barriers to entry and foster a welcoming environment.

```
# Community outreach email snippet
Mentorship Opportunities:
- Open sessions for newcomers every first Friday of the month
- Join our Slack channel for guidance and resources: #linkerd-mentorship
```

This example illustrates proactive steps taken to guide newcomers into the community, ensuring their contributions enrich the ecosystem while they gain valuable experience.

- The Role of CNCF (Cloud Native Computing Foundation)

Linkerd, a flagship project of the CNCF, benefits from shared resources and a thriving ecosystem of complementary technologies. The CNCF offers a support framework for open source projects, aiding with marketing, documentation, and growth insights, which empower Linkerd to network and integrate with other cloud-native projects seamlessly.

```
# CNCF support overview for Linkerd
- Technical oversight and direction
- Infrastructure support (CI/CD systems)
- Sponsorship for community events and summit attendance
```

This overview underscores CNCF's contribution to Linkerd's development, providing the infrastructure and directional support that underpins sustainable growth and system maturity.

## 10.6. COMMUNITY AND OPEN SOURCE CONTRIBUTIONS

- Developing and Sharing Best Practices

  Linkerd's community is instrumental in developing best practices, contributing how-tos, tutorials, and operational guides that inform new users and foster informed decision-making. These resources are invaluable for organizations transitioning to microservices architectures and offer an expanded repertoire of strategies for Linkerd deployments.

  ```
  # Example best practices contribution
  Topic: Optimizing Linkerd for large-scale deployments
  Summary: Tips and tricks for scaling Linkerd in environments with 1,000+
      nodes, focusing on memory management and service mesh segmentation.
  Author: opsguru
  ```

  Such contributions enrich the documentation and knowledge base around Linkerd, enabling users to anticipate and surmount common challenges, thereby enhancing deployment confidence and success.

- Streamlined Contributor Experience

  Streamlining the contributor experience involves providing clear guidelines, adequate tooling, and sufficient documentation that make it easier for new developers to get involved. Linkerd's contribution guide is a testament to this effort, offering clear pathways from beginner questions to advanced feature development.

  ```
  # Contribution guide overview
  Steps:

  1. Fork the repository and clone locally
  2. Set up the Linkerd development environment using 'make' tools
  3. Submit pull requests following the template
  4. Engage in code reviews and resolve feedback
  ```

  These structured steps demystify the contribution process, reducing entry barriers and ensuring continuity in project development by leveraging diverse community expertise.

- Innovation through Hackathons and Meetups

  Linkerd actively participates in organizing and collaborating on hackathons and meetups, which serve as fertile ground for ideation, learning, and collaboration. These events enable community members to connect, share ideas, and prototype solutions rapidly, resulting in significant innovations and improvements on the platform.

```
# Announcement for an upcoming hackathon
Event: Cloud Native Hack 2023
Focus: Building and extending Linkerd integrations
Date: May 15-17
Format: Hybrid (Online and In-Person)
```

Such announcements invite learners, developers, and experts to contribute and innovate in a collaborative setting, often leading to breakthroughs that translate into project enhancement and feature expansion.

- Impact Assessment and Feedback Loops

Regular impact assessments and feedback collection routines are integral to understanding the efficacy of changes made within Linkerd. By closing the feedback loop, the community can iteratively validate and refine features, which proves essential for sustaining relevance and efficacy of Linkerd's functionalities.

```
# Example survey for community feedback
Survey Topic: Linkerd's New Metrics Dashboard
Purpose: Assess usability and identify areas for improvement
Link: [URL]
```

Gathering insights through these surveys enables informed adjustments and fosters a sense of collective progression, ensuring Linkerd evolves in alignment with user expectations and community goals.

Linkerd's commitment to open source principles and community participation empowers it to continuously evolve and adapt to the needs of its users. Through active engagement, transparent governance, and dedicated resources for contributor processes, Linkerd ensures ongoing innovation and resilience. It exemplifies the strength of collective development efforts, whereby diverse contributions and shared expertise drive the project forward, enrich its features, and enhance its global reach, cementing its place as a cornerstone of open source service mesh technologies.

## 10.6. COMMUNITY AND OPEN SOURCE CONTRIBUTIONS

www.ingramcontent.com/pod-product-compliance
Lightning Source LLC
Chambersburg PA
CBHW052144220526
45471CB00004B/1520